BRUCE NARRAMORE

Parenting With Love & Limits

PYRANEE
BOOKS

Zondervan Publishing House
Grand Rapids, Michigan

PARENTING WITH LOVE AND LIMITS
Copyright © 1987 by Bruce Narramore

This volume combines two previously published books:
PARENTING WITH LOVE AND LIMITS
Copyright © 1979 by Bruce Narramore
YOU CAN BE A BETTER PARENT
Copyright © 1979 by Bruce Narramore

Pyranee Books are published by Zondervan Publishing House
1415 Lake Drive, S.E., Grand Rapids, MI 49506

Library of Congress Cataloging in Publication Data
Narramore, Bruce.
    Parenting with love and limits.
    1. Parenting. 2. Religious education. 3. Christian life—
Biblical teaching. I. Title.
HQ755.8.N37   649'.1   79-17873
ISBN 0-310-30541-1

Unless otherwise indicated, scripture quotations taken from the HOLY BIBLE: NEW INTERNATIONAL VERSION (North American Edition) are copyrighted © 1973, 1978, 1984, by The International Bible Society. Used by permission of Zondervan Bible Publishers.

Printed in the United States of America

87 88 89 90 91 92 93 / CH / 10 9 8 7 6 5 4 3 2 1

CONTENTS

75860

ᏢREFACE

I have tried to keep two groups of readers in mind throughout these pages. One is Christian parents—most of whom have already read one or more of the many books available on child rearing. Although they appreciate the insights in these books, many of these parents want to get back to the Bible and discover the scriptural model of parenting. Instead of sampling additional techniques in child training, they want to be certain about the biblical foundation for parenting. With this foundation they can then weigh the conflicting counsel sometimes offered to parents and they can develop ways of interacting with their children that are consistent with this foundation. They will also be able to select other books and materials that can help them to apply these principles to family needs.

Although I have illustrated many concepts with practical applications and examples, this book is not designed primarily to tell parents how to stop temper tantrums, overcome sibling rivalry, resolve eating problems, or handle teen-age conflicts. Instead, it is designed to discover the biblical model of parent-child interaction and to identify basic issues of parenting. In the latter portion of the book I've included a series of exercises to help you apply these biblical principles to your family.

As I wrote this book I also kept in mind pastors, teachers, seminarians, and other Christian leaders who are called to relate the whole counsel of God's Word to this generation. The current crisis in the family exposes a void in our theology curriculum. We have structured theology and theological education in ways that neglect a vast amount of biblical material. The Christian leader who wishes to instruct others in the vital area of child rearing has had little if any preparation. Likely he has not had even one course in the biblical foundation of family living. And if he did, it was probably taught as an elective in the Christian education department rather than as an integral part of his theological training.

Every minister should be familiar with the large body of scriptural truth that relates to the family. It is a major theme of the Bible, and it speaks to some of the most basic needs of man. Is not the nurture of the family one of our highest priorities in the ministry? Here, in struggling with real-life problems and frustrations, we are challenged to prove Scripture relevant and workable. Teaching and preaching on the family gives pastors and teachers a unique opportunity to make doctrine alive and meaningful. And it is one of the best ways to motivate parents to delve into the Word of God.

The text of this volume avoids extensive theoretical discussions or digressions that move beyond the interest of most parents; the notes, which appear at the back of the book, cover areas and resources that may attract pastors, students, and theologians. Readers who are not interested in this technical or theoretical background can skip these notes without missing any of the biblical principles treated in this book.

–1–
THE
𝒫ARENTING
𝒫EVOLUTION

Our generation is witnessing an explosion of literature about the family. Almost weekly new titles are coming off the press. On the bookshelves of my study stand over one hundred volumes on the subject of rearing children! From the secular classic *Baby and Child Care* by Benjamin Spock[1] to the latest treatises from Christian sources, these books span the gamut of styles in parenting. This literature explosion is matched by an equally burgeoning phenomenon—the family seminar movement. Across the country couples are streaming to lectures and workshops designed to teach them how to live meaningfully with their families. To be frank, I view both of these phenomena with mixed emotions.

It is clear that Christian families desperately need help. The alarming increase in divorce, the growing incidence of second-generation "spiritual dropouts," and the general deterioration of family foundations make the developments cited above encouraging. For too long the church has neglected this basic aspect of Christian living. We have either left the parenting task to secular authorities in the fields of education and psychology or we have squeezed instruction into an occasional sermon or Sunday school lesson. At last this deficiency is recognized. Concerned Christians are concentrating on family renewal, seminaries are advancing courses on the family for future church leaders, and many churches now offer at least occasional electives on family living.

In spite of the promising efforts in this "Christian family movement," there are some potentially serious problems. First of all, the advice to parents is conflicting. One author advocates physical correction; another condemns it. One stresses the authority of parents while another promotes children's rights. One expert recommends letting children settle their own squabbles but is later contradicted by someone who urges parents to intervene. This conflicting counsel is confusing. Parents do not know where to turn, and they don't know who to trust. As one parent observed wryly, "If all the experts on rearing children were laid end to end, they would never reach a conclusion!"

Underlying this confusion is a bigger problem. All of us have a tendency to take our own ideas or a popular current philosophy, find a few verses of Scripture that seem to support it, and pass it off as "Christian." This approach frequently yields immediate relief of a problem, but it can also cause serious distortions of the biblical design for parenting.

These books that Christian parents are looking to for advice tend to fall into three categories. First are those written by pastors and other Christian leaders, which are usually edited versions of sermons or conference messages. The author selects a number of Bible passages and scriptural principles and applies them to rearing children.[2]

Many of these books do serve to introduce parents to the resources of Scripture as well as to other tested guidelines and principles for rearing children. However, they tend to have two weaknesses. First, they lack comprehensiveness. Since these books often evolve out of sermon outlines, the authors have had to be selective about their use of Scripture. A dozen thirty-minute sermons cannot begin to touch on all of the Scripture passages that relate to parenting. Consequently, these books neglect or slight many areas of theology that should be brought to bear on rearing children. The second weakness is a tendency to avoid practical guidance and instruction. Because they were intended as sermons or messages for a general audience, they do not address such nitty-gritty issues as how to motivate children to clean their rooms, how to stop sibling fights, or how to handle a rebellious teenager.

The second category of books consists of volumes written by professional psychologists and counselors. More psychological and more practical, these books generally make little or no attempt to present a comprehensive biblical view of parenting. Although they may contain a lot of Scripture, it is for the purpose of illustrating or supporting a psychological thesis or principle rather than to serve as the book's ultimate foundation.[3]

In the third group are the semibiographical accounts of the experiences of Christian laymen with their children. Included here are books and pamphlets such as *Children—Fun or Frenzy?*[4]

These three types of Christian books on parenting, along with the array of books on the same subject by secular authors, make up an impressive, if baffling, assortment for the concerned parent. They offer distinctive helps to beleaguered parents, but they all lack a vital element—they fail to build a comprehensive and systematic framework for rearing children that is firmly grounded in the totality of biblical revelation. I am not aware of one of these books that has endeavored to pull together all of the scriptural principles and insights that relate to rearing children and then present them in a way that is both relevant to parents and theologically consistent. None of them traces the implications of Scripture for parenting by beginning with the facts of creation in Genesis and continuing through the Bible to the end of the Book of Revelation. We are left with a "hit-or-miss" or proof-texting approach to child rearing that neglects much biblical teaching on this crucial topic. This is unfortunate—and potentially dangerous—since the Bible is filled with insights and instructions on the task of parenting. While the Bible is not intended as a textbook on child psychology or child development, it does provide both a solid foundation and systematic framework for rearing children—even in our technological society.

Unfortunately, this deficiency in books for parents is overshadowed by the dearth of information on parenting in theology books. When I examined a half-dozen widely read systematic theology texts, I did not find a single reference to the task of parenting. It was only after I had probed into other sources that I finally found a few.

One of the best was John Gill's *Body of Divinity.*[5] But it was written over two hundred years ago, and its excellent discussion of parenting covers just four pages. A number of brief articles in Bible dictionaries, encyclopedias, and other study books also touch on the topic, but the nearest I found to a theology of parenting was Herbert Lockyer's *All the Children of the Bible.*[6] This excellent book is essentially a compilation of and elaboration on most of the biblical passages that deal directly with children. Yet it does not attempt to give in-depth treatment to issues such as the nature of family government, principles of discipline, the child's self-image, and responsibilities of parents and children.

For some reason we have published hundreds of books on the proper means of baptism, the nature of the church, the doctrine of predestination, and the timing of the Rapture, but we give only superficial treatment to the mass of biblical teachings that relate to rearing children. Yet God's first command to Adam and Eve was to "be fruitful and multiply and replenish the earth." And the Bible contains nearly two thousand references to "child" and "children"!

Yet, all this is understandable. Family-life specialists such as psychologists, psychiatrists, and family counselors generally have little if any formal training in theology. And theologians generally have had little training in as pragmatic a task as rearing children. Unfortunately, the lack of a theology of parenting hurts us all. Parents are left wandering among a maze of conflicting books and theories. Children are left without proper guidance. And our theology suffers from being one-sided. This failure to deal with the task of parenting makes it seem as if God is silent on a crucial issue and as if our theology does not speak to a major area of life. As Gill put it, child rearing is one aspect of our worship. It should be "performed with a respect to God, under His authority, according to His will and command, and in obedience to it, and with a view to His glory."[7] Since it is a vital part of our relationship to God, parenting can no longer remain a secondary concern of theology.

If the present renewal in Christian family living is to take root and bring the changes all of us desire, it must be thoroughly grounded in Scripture. We must move beyond Christian proof-texting and isolated exposition and begin applying the rich resources of the Bible in a more comprehensive and balanced way. We must be willing to think through the implications of our theology for how we are to live together as parents and children.[8]

THE BIBLE
SPEAKS
TO PARENTS

Most Christian parents can recall two or three biblical injunctions about raising children—if hard pressed—but they are nonetheless inclined to think that the Bible gives only sketchy directions for modern parents. This impression is understandable since there are no more than a score or so specific biblical instructions on parenting. And since the Bible does not give a detailed picture of developmental stages nor step-by-step methods for solving all parenting problems, we may wrongly conclude there is insufficient material in Scripture for building a systematic theology of parenting. But if we look beyond the specific commands to parents, we find a storehouse of resources. In fact, there are at least five sources of information and instruction in Scripture for parents.[1]

Commands and Promises to Parents

Since the number of commands and promises to parents is not great, we will list them without comment to show the most apparent biblical teachings on parent-child relations.

> "And when your children ask you, 'What does this ceremony mean to you?' then tell them, 'It is the Passover sacrifice to the LORD who passed over the houses of the

Israelites in Egypt and spared our homes when he struck down the Egyptians.'" (Exod. 12:26-27)

Only be careful and watch yourselves closely so that you do not forget the things your eyes have seen or let them slip from your heart as long as you live. Teach them to your children and to their children after them. (Deut. 4:9)

Hear, O Israel: The LORD our God, the LORD is one. Love the LORD your God with all your heart and with all your soul and with all your strength. These commandments that I give you today are to be upon your hearts. Impress them on your children. . . . (Deut. 6:4-7)

Fix these words of mine in your hearts and minds; tie them as symbols on your hands and bind them on your foreheads. Teach them to your children, talking about them when you sit at home and when you walk along the road, when you lie down and when you get up. (Deut. 11:18-19)

When Moses finished reciting all these words to all Israel, he said to them, "Take to heart all the words I have solemnly declared to you this day, so that you may command your children to obey carefully all the words of this law." (Deut. 32:45-46)

He who spares the rod hates his son,
    but he who loves him is careful to discipline him.
                                    (Prov. 13:24)

Discipline your son, for in that there is hope;
    do not be a willing party to his death.
                                    (Prov. 19:18)

Train a child in the way he should go
    and when he is old he will not turn from it.
                                    (Prov. 22:6)

Folly is bound up in the heart of a child,
    but the rod of discipline will drive it far from him.
                                    (Prov. 22:15)

Do not withhold discipline from a child;
if you punish him with the rod, he will not die.
Punish him with the rod,
and save his soul from death.
(Prov. 23:13-14)

Discipline your son, and he will give you peace;
he will bring delight to your soul.
(Prov. 29:17)

Fathers, do not exasperate your children; instead, bring them up in the training and instruction of the Lord. (Eph. 6:4)

Fathers, do not embitter your children, or they will become discouraged. (Col. 3:21)

Here is a trustworthy saying: If anyone sets his heart on being an overseer, he desires a noble task. . . . He must manage his own family well and see that his children obey him with proper respect. (If anyone does not know how to manage his own family, how can he take care of God's church?) (1 Tim. 3:1, 4-5)

A deacon must be the husband of but one wife and must manage his children and his household well. (1 Tim. 3:12)

If anyone does not provide for his relatives, and especially for his immediate family, he has denied the faith and is worse than an unbeliever. (1 Tim. 5:8)

God Our Parent

Throughout Scripture we also find a rich variety of objects and relationships used to illustrate spiritual truths. Christ spoke of light to describe spiritual illumination (John 8:12). He referred to bread to portray spiritual food (John 6:35). And he described a vine and its branches to illustrate the concept of dependency (John 15:1-8). Perhaps the most beautiful analogy in Scripture is the parallel drawn between the human father and our heavenly Father. Paul quotes from an Old Testament promise of God (2 Sam. 7:14; 7:8) that depicts this parallel: "'I will be a Father to you, and you will be my sons and daughters, says the Lord Almighty'" (2 Cor. 6:18).

Over three thousand times Scripture uses the words "child," "children," "father," and "fathers." The vast majority of these refer to God's relation as father to His convenant people Israel or to His spiritual children. But there is also much here for earthly fathers to learn. We can transfer principles that govern God's relationship with us as His children to our dealings with our children. Richard Strauss observes:

> Isn't it interesting that when Jesus prayed he addressed God as "our Father, who art in heaven"? God is a father. And the Psalmist exclaimed, 'What a God He is. How perfect in every way!' (TLB) The obvious conclusion is that God is a perfect father. By examining His Word and learning how He functions as a parent, we can learn what kind of parents we should be. Then when we commit ourselves completely to Him and let Him control our lives, He is free to express through us His wisdom and strength as the Model Parent. He provides both the example and the encouragement, both the direction and the dynamic for us to be successful parents.[2]

Herbert Lockyer expresses the same truth:

> Our heavenly Father has not left Himself without witness even in the human parenthood on earth. That the earthly relationship is a reflection of the heavenly is borne by our Lord's questions to His own. "If ye, then, being evil, know how to give good gifts unto your children, how much more shall your Father which is in heaven give good things to them that ask Him?" (Matt. 7:11) From the fatherliness of God we can learn a great deal about our parental obligations. As He created man in His image and after His likeness, so our children should be, not only objects of our love, but also a reflection of our godward aspirations. The more the Father/Mother heart of God is understood, the truer and more joyful the parenthood on earth.[3]

Throughout our study we will keep this parallel of God the Father and earthly fathers in mind, but in order to appreciate its power we will take note of five Old Testament passages in which God's fatherhood is pertinent to earthly parents. Exodus 2:23-25 shows that God is sensitive to His children's troubles. In Exodus 3:9-10 He protects His children. In Exodus 6:5-8 and 12:51 He keeps His promises. And in Exodus 16:13-15 God provides for His children. God has given Himself as the example of the perfect parent. If we are to understand our role and responsibilities as parents, we must seek to understand the nature, attributes, and works of God.[4] This, then, is our second source for building a systematic biblical approach to child rearing.

Our Human Nature

The Bible also abounds with God's revelation about the nature, qualities, and character of the human race.[5] Even when not addressed specifically to parents or children, passages that elaborate on the basic elements of human nature have a direct bearing on a theology of parenting. They speak to the needs of people, the effects of sin, and the necessity of discipline and correction. These passages provide a biblical frame of reference for considering many practical issues in child rearing, and they enable us to evaluate the conflicting counsel given to parents today. For example, behavioristic philosophies, which claim that all actions are determined by our environment, contradict the biblical teaching that each person is created in the image of God and is responsible for his or her choices and decisions. And the humanistic belief in the essential goodness of humanity, which leads to permissive or democratic views of child rearing, is not consistent with Scripture.

Throughout our study of the parent-child relationship we will frequently refer to the biblical view of human nature and human personality.

Family Examples

The fourth source for a theology of parenting comes from the many narratives in the Bible about parents and their children. For example, Abraham, Isaac, and Jacob give a three-generation picture of the transmission of a father's sin (in this case, lying) to successive generations (Gen. 12:10-13; 20:1-5; 26:6-11; 27:1-46). Joseph and his brothers provide insight into the problem of parental favoritism (Gen. 37–45). David and his children show the bitter fruits of several sins, including adultery and murder (2 Sam. 11–18). And Timothy, his mother, and grandmother are an example of the power of a positive parental influence (2 Tim. 1:5). Although we cannot cover all biblical portrayals of parenting we will examine many for illumination and for clarification of the divine pattern of parenting.

Counsel on Relationships

Our final source of information for a theology of parenting is the great amount of Scripture dealing with interpersonal relationships. The Bible is filled with counsel on our relationships with others, and most of these passages contain principles that apply directly to our relationships with children. Here are a few examples:

> A gentle answer turns away wrath,
> but a harsh word stirs up anger.
> (Prov. 15:1)

> He who answers before listening—
> that is his folly and his shame.
> (Prov. 18:13)

> "A new commandment I give you: Love one another. As I have loved you, so you must love one another." (John 13:34)

> Brothers, if someone is caught in a sin, you who are spiritual should restore him gently. But watch yourself, or you also may be tempted. Carry each other's burdens, and in this way you will fulfill the law of Christ. (Gal. 6:1-2)

> Therefore each of you must put off falsehood and speak truthfully to his neighbor, for we are all members of one body. (Eph. 4:25)

> Therefore confess your sins to each other and pray for each other so that you may be healed. The prayer of a righteous man is powerful and effective. (James 5:16)

Although these Scripture verses are not addressed explicitly to parents, they certainly apply to the intimacies of the parent-child relationship. In the family, as well as elsewhere, we see that: anger stirs up strife but a soft answer relieves conflict; listening and honesty are healing virtues; and we should bear one another's burdens and correct one another gently when we sin. It is bewildering that many parents who are committed to these biblical truths rarely think of applying them in their relationships with their own children!

With this survey of the portions of Scripture that relate to rearing children, we can see that many of the verses in the Bible have implications for parents. From the opening chapter of Genesis to the close of the Book of Revelation, there is a wealth of guidance that speaks directly to the needs of parents and their children. It is critical for today's Christian families to recognize this divine resource and to delve into God's treasures of wisdom for child rearing.

– 3 –

PURPOSES
OF
PARENTING

Most parents want immediate help with problems of daily living. They're looking for advice on how to handle temper tantrums, eating problems, communication obstacles, bedtime hassles, and a host of other common frustrations. These concerns are certainly valid, but they can obscure more vital needs and issues. If we focus too exclusively on these "practical" concerns, we are apt to neglect the major purposes of parenting and fail to perceive God's divine plan.

Christian families need to recognize that the family is a sacred institution. While we cannot ignore the routine matters of daily life, we must not forget that God has given the design for family living. He instituted the family as the first unit of society, and throughout Scripture it is central to His working in the world.

To understand this design and God's plans for parenthood, we must first consider the purpose of creation. Why, in the ages past, did God step into time, create the universe, and populate this planet with human beings? Until we answer this question we lack a frame of reference for fully understanding the parent-child relationship. We may focus on individual problems, conflicts, or ideals, but we will fail to see the grand design that is the basis for the family achieving its full potential. Apart from this understanding, we may be problem solvers, but we will not be full-fledged partners in God's great plan of the ages.

Glorifying God

Scripture testifies that God created the universe to manifest His glory and His character. The apostle Paul asserts the sovereignty of God and the righteousness of His choices when he speaks of God choosing Jacob but not Esau. Then Paul recalls that God hardened the heart of the pharaoh who was oppressing the descendants of Jacob and he asks:

> What if God, choosing to show his wrath and make his power known, bore with great patience the objects of his wrath—prepared for destruction? What if he did this to make the riches of his glory known to the objects of his mercy, whom he prepared in advance for glory? (Rom. 9:23-24)

This illustration from history is balanced by equally clear prophetic statements of God's purpose. Isaiah writes:

> Bring my sons from afar
>   and my daughters from the ends of the earth—
> everyone who is called by my name,
>   whom I created for my glory,
>   whom I formed and made.
>   (Isa. 43:6-7)

There are many other passages such as this that speak of God's basic purpose in the world.[1]

Throughout the Old and New Testament alike we read that God created to manifest His glory. This statement, however, upsets some people. It conjures up pictures of a selfish, proud, or manipulative God who is interested only in Himself. Before we can get excited about participating in God's great plan, we must understand the meaning and significance of the glory of God.

God's glory is not like our self-seeking glory. His glory is not something external. It is not God building up His esteem of Himself. And it is not something that detracts from the significance of others. God's attributes of holiness (1 Sam. 2:2; Isa. 57:15; Hos. 11:9), wisdom (Ps. 33:10-11; Rom. 11:33; Eph. 3:10), truthfulness (Num. 23:19; 1 Cor. 1:9; 2 Tim. 2:13), goodness (Ps. 145:2-9; Matt. 6:26; Acts 14:17), and love (Rom. 9:15-16; Eph. 1:6; 1 Peter 3:20; 1 John 4:8), are glorious in themselves. For God to demonstrate these attributes is not a selfish quest for glory; it is His expression of His true nature. To be true to His nature God must exercise His power, His righteousness, and His love. And because God is true to His nature, all of creation participates in His glory. As theologian Augustus Strong put it:

> His own glory is an end which comprehends and secures, as a subordinate end, every interest of the universe. The interests of the universe are bound up in the interests of God. There is no holiness or happiness for creatures except as God is absolutely sovereign, and is recognized as such. It is therefore not selfishness, but benevolence, for God to make his own glory the supreme object of creation. Glory is not vain-glory, and in expressing his ideal, that is, in expressing himself, in his creation, he communicates to his creatures the utmost possible good.[2]

In creating the universe and mankind, God was demonstrating His character and His glory. And He intended mankind to participate in that glory and to be a reflector of it.

> It was His will that man on earth was to have points of resemblance to his Creator, and to prove in all his character and conduct that he was indeed created in God's image. In the domination he was to have over the earth, man was to exhibit the sovereignty and power of God as the King and Ruler of the universe.[3]

With this magnificent divine design in mind, we come to the purpose of the family. The family was God's first and foremost institution to fulfill His purpose in the world. From the creation of Eve, recorded in Genesis 1, through the last chapter of the Book of Revelation, Scripture uses the family to illustrate and demonstrate spiritual truth. Lockyer states:

> In the creation of home life on earth, with its love of
> husband and wife, parent and child, God designed to
> represent the love and blessedness of His home in
> heaven. At the heart of creation was His purpose to
> people the earth with human beings through whom the
> fulness of His love might flow out.[4]

If God's purpose is to communicate His glory through creation, then the primary purpose of the family is to be a vehicle
in this process. And if the family is to communicate God's
glory, family members must be experiencing that glory. In
other words, the family should be instrumental in promoting
righteousness among its members because God is glorified
when His character is reproduced in His children.

When we open Scripture, this is exactly what we find. The
author of Hebrews states that the discipline of God and of our
earthly fathers is designed to produce righteousness.

> Moreover, we have all had human fathers who disci-
> plined us and we respected them for it. How much more
> should we submit to the Father of our spirits and live!
> Our fathers disciplined us for a little while as they
> thought best; but God disciplines us for our good, that
> we may share in his holiness. No discipline seems pleas-
> ant at the time, but painful. Later on, however, it pro-
> duces a harvest of righteousness and peace for those who
> have been trained by it. (Heb. 12:9-11)

The primary goal of child rearing, therefore, is to produce
godly character in children so that God will be glorified. This
perspective transforms the task of child rearing. Our goal is no
longer merely to resolve family conflicts and find a little
peace. Now we are participating in God's great program of the
ages. We are shaping lives for eternity. We are helping to
form each child's character so that he or she reflects God's
glory.

Replenishing and Ruling the Earth

Closely tied to glorifying God is the second purpose of
parenting. God's first command to Adam and Eve was: "Be
fruitful and increase in number; fill the earth and subdue it.

Rule over the fish of the sea and the birds of the air and over every living creature that moves on the ground" (Gen. 1:28).

God directed His image-bearers to produce children and to exercise dominion over the world. Unfortunately, many Christians have lost sight of these twin purposes. We have focused so much on sin, salvation, and eternal life that we have overlooked God's plan for the present. Humankind was placed on earth to rule. Erich Sauer puts it this way:

> God set man on the earth He had prepared for him. He planted the wonderful garden in Eden which was to be the joy and delight of its possessor. Paradise was the beginning of the ways of God with man. God's wisdom, love and power wished to unfold itself in everything on the earth and change everything here below into an ever-blossoming paradise. In man, as the crown of creation, all the blessings planned by His grace were to be brought together and perfectly exhibited. In him, the one free and moral creature on earth, God's moral nature wished to glorify itself and to make man an image of his eternal creator.[5]

This truth impacts every area of life. It means that the mastery of our universe by means of technology should not be minimized, because it plays a part in our dominion over the earth. It means that we should encourage our children to develop and to achieve. And it means that the process of bearing and rearing children is part of God's plan to produce righteousness in the world. This understanding of replenishing and ruling the earth gives parents perspective and direction.

Bringing Joy to Parents

As we unfold the mysteries of creation, we find that whatever accomplishes God's purposes also fulfills human needs. This confirms that God is not selfish in demonstrating His glory and in demanding our worship. God created the human personality so that there is no conflict between man's fulfillment and God's glory. In creating the family to glorify Him and to rule and replenish the earth, God also designed it to produce fulfillment, joy, and blessing. Throughout Scripture children are portrayed as gifts from God.

Psalms 127 and 128 call up the joy that children can create within the family by presenting a four-fold description. In Psalm 127 children are described as "a heritage of the LORD" (v. 3), "a reward" (v. 3), and "arrows" in a man's quiver (vv. 4, 5). And Psalm 128:3 speaks of "olive shoots." We are also told that we will prosper if we love God, and that we will see our children's children (128:5-6). Other Old Testament passages bring together God's delight in us as His children and our delight in our children (Isa. 62:4-5; Prov. 3:12).

Moreover, according to Scripture, children are not to be taken for granted. We read of Isaac asking for a child in behalf of Rebekah (Gen. 25:21). Rachel told Jacob she had to have a child or she would die (Gen. 30:1). When Esau welcomed his long-absent brother Jacob he asked, "Who are these with you?" Jacob replied, "They are the children God has graciously given your servant" (Gen. 33:5). And we read of Hannah pleading with God for a son (1 Sam. 1).

God responds to the cries of those who love Him. He promised the aged Abraham that he and Sarah would have a son and that Sarah would become a "mother of nations" (Gen. 17:16). And an angel came to tell Zechariah that he and Elizabeth would have a son (Luke 1).

How sad that many parents are unable to enjoy their children. Instead of creating happiness, children become the focus of a storm center of conflict that produces great disappointment and frustration. But this needn't be. Parents can enjoy their children.

Models of the Heavenly Parent

As we saw earlier, the Bible draws numerous parallels between earthly fathers and God our heavenly father. This brings us to a fourth purpose of parenting: in establishing the family God has provided a visible model of the way in which He relates to us. In other words, God designed the family to teach us in a tangible, first-hand way about Himself. Just as

God uses the intimate relationship of husband and wife to illustrate Christ's relationship to the church (Eph. 5:22-33), children and parents represent our relationship to Him our heavenly parent (Heb. 12:5-11). Although frequently overlooked, this is one of the most important purposes of the family. Children need experience with flesh-and-blood parents to help them grasp the spiritual truth that God is our heavenly Father.

Richard Strauss puts it this way:

> The point is well established in the Bible. God's parenthood and our parenthood are a great deal alike—at least they should be. . . . A person's image of God is often patterned after his image of his own parents, especially his father. If his parents were happy, loving, accepting, and forgiving, he finds it easier to experience a positive and satisfying relationship with God. But if his parents were cold and indifferent, he may feel that God is far away and disinterested in him personally. If his parents were angry, hostile, and rejecting he often feels that God can never accept him. If his parents were hard to please, he usually has the nagging notion that God is not very happy with him either.[6]

Orphans and children of parents with seriously defective personalities often find it extremely difficult to develop a true conception of God. And if such children do gain an intellectual understanding of the character of God, they frequently have difficulty experiencing the fact that God loves them because their experience with earthly parents was so far removed from the biblical revelation concerning parent-child relations. Even children from "normal" or "healthy" homes are likely to have some false concepts of who God is, since we all fall short of God's character in some degree.

One of the highest callings of Christian parents, then, is to build loving, sensitive, and honest relationships with their children so that later in life these children can freely turn to God the Father and readily accept His loving forgiveness.[7]

What an incentive this is for parents to grow! Although our problems and sins may interfere with our child's relationship with God, our consistent love lays a foundation for meaningful faith in God. Chapter 9 in this volume is a discussion of God's character and our responsibility for communicating effectively His true character.

Providing for Children's Needs

After God created Adam and Eve and gave them dominion over nature, He said: "I give you every seed-bearing plant on the face of the whole earth and every tree that has fruit with seed in it. They will be yours for food" (Gen. 1:29).

This verse makes it clear that God provides for His children's needs. Every plant and every tree were to provide food for Adam and Eve. Just as God provided companionship for Adam (Gen. 2:18), so too the plants and trees were provisions for the physical needs of Adam and Eve.

In the New Testament Paul tells us: "My God will meet all your needs according to his glorious riches in Christ Jesus" (Phil. 4:19). What better reminder of a parent's responsibility to provide could there be than God supplying our needs?

Giving Training and Instruction

A final purpose of parenting is to provide the training, instruction, and correction needed by all children if they are to mature spiritually, socially, and intellectually. The most familiar biblical principle of child rearing instructs us to "train a child in the way he should go" (Prov. 22:6). Since this function is so evident and since we will develop specific principles of training in chapter 6, we will go on after simply asserting that in properly training our children we are fulfilling one of God's divine purposes for parenting.

The six purposes of parenting mentioned briefly in this chapter, when rightly understood, can bring radical changes in parents' attitudes toward children. Child rearing can be changed from a tedious, frustrating task to an enjoyable opportunity with lasting spiritual importance. While this perspective won't solve all of our problems, it goes a long way in providing a firm foundation for positive parent-child relations.

-4-

ᏑᎯMILY
ᏋLEADERSHIP

Probably the most controversial issue concerning parenting is the question of family leadership or family government. Most families give the matter little attention—they simply follow their instincts or respond to the strongest immediate influence. But every family practices some form of "government" in every-day living. This issue divides experts and parents alike, and it influences nearly every facet of the parent-child relationship. It determines methods of discipline, attitudes toward communication, our approach to a child's self-esteem, and many other issues.

Styles of family government range along a continuum from the authoritarian to the permissive. The authoritarian style emphasizes power, punishment, and pressure. Parents here are unquestioned authorities whose job it is to control children and force them into desired behavior. Listen to an extreme representative of this approach:

> Take a walnut. Now pick up a nutcracker. Insert the nut and squeeze . . . crraaacckk! That's the way to handle a rebellious teen. Put him in the nutcracker and squeeze. Something will give—you can be sure of that. Can't you see the shell of that walnut crumbling under the pres-

sure of those jaws? Well, that's what happens to your boy or girl when you follow the plan set forth in this book.[1]

Parents following an authoritarian model typically make heavy use of physical punishment. They set themselves up as the ones to decide what's best for the child, and they do not allow their authority to be challenged. They are quick to tell their children what to do and are slow to listen. They do not allow their children to have a voice in decision making. When their children disobey, these parents don't try to understand the forces behind the problem nor do they explore sensitively their child's feelings. They want the misbehavior to stop— "and now!" Their motto is "Fight power with power!"

At the other end of the continuum, the permissive style emphasizes self-determination. Pressure and force are out of the question because children should be allowed to develop according to their own interests and choices. Under labels such as "progressive education," "democracy," and "child-centered homes," this philosophy dominated child rearing and educational practice in the 1940s.

John Dewey in education, Carl Rogers in psychology, and Benjamin Spock in pediatrics were leaders of the movement. They attacked authoritarian parenting and offered a child-centered view in its place. At the core of this "new" attitude was the belief that children could make good choices on their own and direct their own lives with very little outside interference. A. S. Neill, author of the controversial book *Summerhill,* is one of the most outspoken proponents of this perspective. Neill writes: "I believe that to impose anything by authority is wrong. The child shouldn't do anything until he comes to the opinion—his own opinion—that it should be done."[2]

Between the extremes of authoritarianism and permissiveness we find many other styles of family government, and each of these is the result of three factors. The first is the parent's own upbringing: that is, authoritarian parents tend to produce authoritarian parents, and permissive parents produce permissive parents. The second source of parenting style is the culture: parents tend to rear children according to the prevailing model of the day. If that model is authoritarian (as it generally was until the middle of the twentieth century), parents tend to rear their children in an authoritarian manner. If the prevailing model is permissive (as it was in much of the United States in the 1940s and 1950s), most children are reared in a permissive manner. But there is a deeper and even more basic source: Our style of parenting flows logically from our view of human nature. Every style of family government and every approach to child rearing is rooted in a philosophy of life that contains a certain view of human nature.

Human Nature and Family Government

If children are viewed as being basically sinners, we are led logically to an authoritarian style of family government. Rebels and sinners need to be controlled and punished. We can allow little freedom and few choices because they are sinners to the core of their being. The parents' prime responsibility is restriction and refinement of this sinful inclination. Larry Christenson expresses this perspective.

> Since the time of the French Revolution the idea has gained wide acceptance that human nature is basically good. The "evil" that crops out from time to time is due to lack of education and understanding, or perhaps from psychological patterns inflicted by one's background and environment. What is needed, we are told, is education and perhaps some adjustment in one's environment— economic, social, political, psychological. Once a person "understands" and once artificial restrictions have been removed, the innate goodness of human nature will burst into flower. The Bible comes at the business of child-raising from a fundamentally different point of view. The Bible does not look upon a child as basically good! "Behold, I was brought forth in iniquity, and in sin my mother conceived me" (Ps. 51:5). The Bible does not view a child as one who essentially wants to do the wise and right thing. Its understanding of the child's nature is different and therefore its approach to discipline is different.[3]

With this as a frame of reference, he goes on to present the one form of discipline he believes to be consistent with his view of children—the rod. In a section titled "The Rod: God's Appointed Means of Discipline," he writes:

> Parents will never have a clear-cut approach to the discipline of their children until they accept the rod as God's appointed means of discipline. It is the choice of His wisdom and His fatherly love. When a parent finds himself shirking the responsibility which God gives him at this point, shirking from it because of his own feelings or reasonings, let him set God's Word above his own feelings and reason: "Do not withold discipline from a child; if you beat him with a rod, he will not die. If you beat him with a rod you will save his life from hell!" (Prov. 23:13-14).[4]

Since Christenson views children as essentially evil and rebellious, he emphasizes physical punishment and control. It is true that the Bible teaches that human nature is sinful already at birth and also endorses corporal punishment, but later we will see that Scripture sees the person as much more than merely sinner and discipline as much broader than the rod alone.

If, in contrast to seeing them as basically evil, children are viewed as essentially good (or at least morally neutral), we are led naturally to a permissive (or at least democratic) view of family government. Proponents of this view insist that, left to their own devices and given sufficient love, children will mature into responsible adults. There is little or no need for parents to exercise authority. Neill puts it bluntly: "Self-regulation implies a belief in the goodness of human nature; a belief that there is not, and never was, original sin."[5] So Neill believes in the innate goodness of human nature, and he proceeds logically to a totally permissive view of child rearing.

Jean Jacques Rousseau, the eighteenth-century French philosopher, and Henry David Thoreau, the nineteenth-century American naturalist, were two prominent spokesmen for this optimistic view of human nature. Both of these men rejected the biblical teaching of original sin; they believed human nature was innocent and good. They attributed man's dilemma to "society" and proposed a return to nature as a panacea. In their view, child rearing should not contain the impositions of society (including those of the parents); it should follow instead the innocence of nature.

Rousseau's *Émile*, published in 1762, was one of the first strong attacks on the concepts of human sinfulness and authoritarian parenting. According to Rousseau, childhood should be a happy time, play should be encouraged, and the word *obey* should be removed from the child's vocabulary. The child should learn to do the proper thing in order to avoid painful consequences, but not for the purpose of obeying an adult.

Rousseau wrote that children "should never act from obedience but only from necessity. For this reason, the words 'obey' and 'command' must be banished from his vocabulary, still more the words 'duty' and 'obligation.'"[6] And he goes on to say: "Let us lay it down as an incontestable principle that the first impulses of nature are always right. There is no original perversity in the human heart. Of every vice we say how it entered and whence it came."[7]

Rousseau and Thoreau left their imprint on current students of child development such as Rudolf Dreikurs, Arnold Gesell, and Thomas Gordon. Dreikurs's commitment to a democratic view of family government and his use of natural consequences are directly traceable to the influence of Rousseau.[8] In fact, the vast majority of secular authors on parenting promote this optimistic view of human nature.

Dreikurs issues a very persuasive call for this democratic style of parenting:

> Children sense the democratic atmosphere of our times and resent our attempts at authority over them. They show their resentment through retaliations. We must become very much aware of our new role as leaders and give up completely our ideas of authority. We simply do not have authority over our children. They know it even if we don't. We can no longer demand or impose. We must learn to lead and how to stimulate.[9]

Thomas Gordon, founder of the popular Parent Effectiveness Training movement, looks back into history and assesses the authoritarian approach as follows:

> The stubborn persistence of the idea that parents must and should use authority in dealing with children has, in my opinion, prevented for centuries any significant change or improvement in the way children are raised by parents and treated by adults.[10]

The widespread popularity of these views calls for a careful evaluation in the light of Scripture. If we accept the biblical teaching that children are sinful, then it also follows that they need parental guidance, direction, and correction. Later in this chapter we will look at specific problems in authoritarian and permissive styles of parenting, but first we will take a closer look at the biblical view of human nature and its implications for family government.

Children as Image Bearers

Theologian Louis Berkhof pinpoints the biblical view of the first aspect of human nature when he states: "The Bible represents man as the crown of God's handiwork, whose special glory consists in this—that he is created in the image of God and after His likeness (Gen. 1:26-27)."[11] With this premise we begin our study of the biblical view of human nature.

We must take care to begin where God began, and the first thing that God reveals about human nature is that people are made in His likeness. Unless we go back to this foundation we hold an incomplete and inaccurate picture. And if the person with whom we begin is anything less than a creature fashioned in the likeness of God, we cannot go on to an understanding of the true nature of children nor can we come to appreciate the nurture that allows for their wholesome maturation.

Clearly the image of God in man is not physical resemblance. The Gospel of John tells us that "God is Spirit, and his worshipers must worship in spirit and in truth" (4:24). In the words of theologian Henry C. Thiessen, we possess a mental, moral, and social likeness to God.[12]

Like God, we possess extraordinary mental gifts. We are able to reason, plan, reflect, and innovate. For example, God gave Adam the formidable task of naming every living creature (Gen. 2:19-20). Adam and Eve's dominion over the world included the realm of the intellect.

Like God, we have a moral nature. After creating Adam and Eve, God saw that His creation was "very good" (Gen. 1:31), without flaw and without any trace of evil. The Book of Ecclesiastes tells us that "God made mankind upright" (7:29). This moral excellence included an affinity to the good and toward God—though this was defiled by rebellion.

Like God, we humans are also social beings. Just as God showers His love on His creatures and develops a relationship with those who respond to Him, every human being seeks companionship and yearns to love others.

The fact that each person bears the image of God has at least three implications for a theology of parenting. First, it attests to each person's significance and value. The psalmist exults because we are made "a little lower than [God] and crowned with glory and honor" (Ps. 8:5), and James warns us not to curse men because they bear the image of God (3:9).

This biblical view of human nature raises the child to the highest level of significance and value. B. B. Warfield writes that "childhood owes as much to the gospel as [does] womanhood itself."[13] Jesus was indignant when the disciples turned away little children: "Let the little children come to me, and do not hinder them for the kingdom of God belongs to such as these" (Mark 10:14).[14]

Each person's right to self-esteem is rooted in the first chapters of Scripture, and it continues as a theme throughout the remainder of the Bible. Parents honor God by teaching each one of their children that he or she is the apex of God's wondrous creation—a unique individual made for eternal companionship with the Almighty.

The second implication of bearing the image of God pertains to the abilities and gifts of children. Every child is born with enormous talent and potential; he or she possesses all sorts of qualities and skills. Psalm 139 contains a fascinating description of how God fashions every human being.

> For you created my inmost being;
>   you knit me together in my mother's womb.
> I praise you because I am fearfully and wonderfully
>   made;
>   your works are wonderful,
>   I know that full well.
> My frame was not hidden from you
>   when I was made in the secret place.
> When I was woven together in the depths of the earth,
>   your eyes saw my unformed body.
> All the days ordained for me
>   were written in your book
>   before one of them came to be.
>   (Ps. 139:13-16)

God is described as the architect and midwife of every person's soul and body. His craftsmanship produces a creature with an unimaginable reservoir of capabilities.

Third, the image of God establishes each person's identity. As Francis Schaeffer puts it, "As I look at myself in the flow of space-time reality, I see my origin in Adam and in God's creating man in His own image."[15] We know that neither the ape nor chance is our link with ultimate reality; we are made by the hand of God, through Adam, in the spiritual mode of the supreme being.

These qualities of the child as image-bearer of God—intrinsic significance, possession of gifts and capabilities, and heavenly foundation for identity—speak eloquently to parents. They declare that the child has a right to be respected; they assert the child's unique individuality and worth; and they trace our children's origin to God.

Abuses of Authority

The fact that children are divine image-bearers argues against an authoritarian form of family government. Authoritarianism, with its one-sided emphasis on external conformity, a child's sinfulness, and the idea that "children should be seen and not heard," runs counter to the biblical teaching that children are significant. Authoritarianism suffers from at least four major faults.

First, it requires the presence of an authority to keep the child in line. It is well-known but frequently ignored that "When the cat's away the mice will play." Some of the most mischievous children are those whose parents try to control them through anger, force, and pressure. As soon as parents get out of sight, bedlam reigns.

Second, authoritarianism, with its reliance on power and fear as motivators, prevents the child from developing a set of love-motivated controls. Since children in an authoritarian home shape their conduct to avoid punishment, they lack incentive to develop their own inner values. They conform, not because it is good for them or for others, but because they are afraid to do otherwise.

A third problem of authoritarianism is that it stunts psychological growth and fosters immature dependency. If children do not rebel against the rigid control exercised in an authoritarian home, they will succumb to mindless conformity. They will blindly follow the wishes of their parents and others, while at the same time losing touch with their own individuality, spontaneity, and flexibility. Instead of learning to confront difficult decisions with their own resources, they respond mechanically according to an imposed code of conduct. By adhering tightly to this code, they avoid the twin risks of options that require a decision and consequences that such a decision sets into motion. Even as adults, they cling to the standards and teachings of their parents because they have proven neither their own adequacy nor their own ability to make decisions.

The final difficulty in authoritarian parenting is its negative effect on a child's self-esteem. Parents who dominate and pressure their children and who do not respect their capacities and gifts undermine the child's attempts to gain confidence and to develop self-esteem. The child feels bad and sinful. Lacking self-respect, he or she is forced into passive identification with the parents in order to gain a sense of significance or to rebel in an attempt to gain recognition and admiration. In either case, these children will likely suffer nagging doubts about their worth and value.

Many parents use authoritarian methods to rear their children with few ill effects surfacing before the adolescent years. Then, as the young person's desire for personal identity and responsibility awakens, the bankruptcy of authoritarianism is exposed. Neither parent nor teen is prepared to discuss areas of conflict and disagreement. The parent is used to telling rather than listening and sharing, but the teen-ager is no longer content with this arrangement. Only if the parents are able to "shift gears" and listen will they have any influence in helping the child to navigate the swirling currents of these turbulent years.

Children as Sinners

Of course, being made in the image of God is only one part of human nature. Shortly after being created in God's image, Adam and Eve rebelled against God (Gen. 3:6-13).

As soon as our first parents disobeyed God, evil and error infected the human race. The image of God was marred, and human nature was spiritually crippled. The sinner was no longer attuned to God, to mate, or to self. In fact, every area of human life was negatively affected by the Fall. The human being's physical, emotional, moral, intellectual, and social make-up was corrupted. No longer would Adam and Eve be free of illness. No longer would they enjoy full harmony with one another. No longer would their reason be flawless. And no longer would their moral drive be selfless. Not long after this first sin, we read the first instance of sibling rivalry and murder.

Adam and Eve's sin did not entirely destroy the image of God in His creatures, but severe damage had been done. The effect of this damage is passed on to every descendant of these first parents. Every person has been born with a disposition toward sin.[16] Any denial or depreciation of this fact, whether it be in the form of Pelagian heresy of the fifth century A.D.[17]

or the humanistic philosophy of the twentieth century, inhibits a proper understanding of humanity and its needs.

The Bible clearly establishes that the effect of Adam's sin has been transmitted to every member of the human race. David writes, "Surely I have been a sinner from birth, sinful from the time my mother conceived me" (Ps. 58:3). And Paul states, "Sin entered the world through one man, and death through sin, and in this way death came to all men, because all sinned" (Rom. 5:12). Even the infant lying in the crib has a natural inclination to sin and a capacity for ultimate rebellion.

Moreover, every person, according to God's Word, exercises this inherent disposition. Isaiah writes, "We all, like sheep, have gone astray, each of us has turned to his own way" (Isa. 53:6). And Paul says, "There is no one righteous, not even one" (Rom. 3:10).

This sinfulness of humankind is the ultimate basis for rejecting both the permissive and democratic style of family government. Scripture makes it clear that children need parental correction and training to help them overcome the power of sin within them. We are told: "Folly is bound up in the heart of a child, but the rod of discipline will drive it far from him" (Prov. 22:15). And in no uncertain terms, God through Paul orders children to obey their parents (Eph. 6:1; Col. 3:20).

The universality of sin and its serious impact on everyday life must not obscure the fact that it is an intruder in human personality. We have fallen from a high destiny, but the plunge is reversible. According to Scripture, we retain the likeness of God despite Adam's fall into sin (Ps. 8:5-8; 1 Cor. 11:7; James 3:9).

Many parents miss this fact. They are unaware of the amazing gifts, capabilities, and potential that are inherent in their children. They understand depravity to mean that sinners are devoid of all capacities and gifts and that they are without worth or value.[18] This leads to rigid control, excessive pressure, and a minimizing of the individuality and worth of the child.

It is easy for a parent who is prone toward an authoritarian style of family government to focus on the sinfulness of their children to the exclusion of their possession of God's image. Such imbalance dishonors the rich endowments that God implanted in Adam and in all his descendants.

The Dangers of Permissiveness

This sinfulness of humankind leads us away from permissive and democratic forms of government, just as the possession of God's image guards us against authoritarianism. While democratic family government is an improvement over the complete lack of control espoused in extreme permissiveness, the fact that these styles rest on the same philosophical foundation warrants their treatment as one. We can cite five problems with this approach to rearing children.

The most serious deficiency of the permissive and democratic views of family government is that they are based on an inadequate view of human nature. Only ignorance of Scripture, blindness to history, or callousness to evil can account for the belief that children need no external controls or parental direction. Second, such freedom from restraint leads the child into actions and patterns with delayed but nonetheless harmful consequences. Third, if parents fail to discipline, this makes it more difficult for children to learn to respect other authority. Fourth, if children do not learn to control their impulses and respect authority during childhood, they are unlikely to learn it later in life. Finally, the lack of adequate structure and parental authority can adversely affect a child's self-esteem.

One researcher recently found that children with the highest level of self-esteem typically come from homes characterized by (1) parental warmth, (2) respect for the child, and (3) reasonable controls.[19] His findings, contrary to the expectations of proponents of a democratic style of family government, underscore the fact that reasonable limits, set and carried out in love, provide a sense of security and a feeling of being loved. We see that permissiveness, in its drive to elevate children to a position of respect and dignity, places too great a burden on young children when it expects them to set their own direction. The lack of a firm and loving parent deprives the child of an essential foundation for security and development.

Parents as Sinners and Image-bearers

Before we trace out the biblical model of family government, we need to look at one more aspect of the picture. According to Scripture, parents as well as children possess both the image of God and an inclination to sin. Adults, too, are drawn simultaneously upward and downward.

On the one hand, the Bible indicates that there is a natural inclination toward positive parenting. For example, Isaiah writes: "As a mother comforts her child, so I will comfort you" (Isa. 66:13).

Solomon, in settling a dispute between two women, relied on the strong love of a mother for her infant child (1 Kings 3). The women were prostitutes and each had an infant son, but one of the boys had died during the night. One woman claimed that the other had exchanged the babies. The other claimed this wasn't true.

Solomon settled the dispute by ordering that the child still alive be cut in half. The real mother protested and offered to withdraw her claim to the child, but the other woman agreed with the king's solution. Solomon then knew who was the real mother, and he ordered that the child be given to her.

Although this passage is primarily an illustration of God's response to Solomon's request for wisdom, it also reveals the strong, innate commitment of a mother to her child. This mother was willing to have her son reared by another woman in order to spare his life! This passage, as well as others, indicates that parents do possess many innate constructive attitudes toward children and toward child rearing. There is some truth in the approach represented by the question: "Isn't it best for parents to do what comes naturally?" Most parents do love their children, sacrifice for their welfare, and respond sensitively to their needs and wishes.

Once again, however, this is only half of the picture. Parents are also inveterate sinners. We are warned, for example, not to provoke our children to wrath (Eph. 6:4; Col. 3:21). Israel's priest, Eli, had to be rebuked for failing to properly train his children (1 Sam. 2:27-36). Sometimes sins such as mistreating our children come just as "naturally" as positive parenting. Parents, too, need guidance and correction in their child rearing.

Scriptural teachings on man's sinfulness speak to the issue of leadership. They caution us against any form of family leadership that sets parents up as gods who possess the authority to run every part of our children's lives. This is the tendency in authoritarian families; the parents' will is not to be questioned and children are to obey "because I said so." There is no sense of mutuality here between the parent and child.

This approach overlooks the fact that while parents do possess valid authority over their children, it is limited by responsibility to God and by the need to respond to another person who, though younger in years, is also made in the image of God. In a very real sense parent and child have similar status. Both are fallible and both can be instruments of God. Effective parents will keep in mind that they too are prone to sin and need to depend on God for constant guidance in rearing their children.

The Biblical Model of Family Government

With this background on the biblical blueprint of man, we are ready to focus on Scripture's view of family government. We have seen that being created in God's image speaks to a child's right to significance and self-esteem and that all children have gifts, potential, and a basis for identity. We have also seen that a child's innate sinfulness implies that there is a need for training and correction.

Aligning the biblical view of human nature with other scriptural teachings on parenting, we are pointed to a structure of family government quite different from either the permissive or authoritarian forms. It is what I term "loving" or "benevolent" authority. Other specialists have called it an authoritative (as opposed to authoritarian) form of leadership. The characteristics of benevolent authority in the family are:

1. Deep respect for each child as an image-bearer and creation of the living God
2. Sensitivity to the unique needs and capabilities of each child
3. Commitment to provide for the needs of the child
4. Delegated authority exercised by parents as a trust from God
5. Keen awareness of the parents' own sinfulness, fallibility, and need of grace
6. Sensitive establishment of necessary limits and guidelines
7. Training and correction based on biblical injunctions
8. Warm and loving family atmosphere

In the following chapters we will spell out in some detail the practical outworking of this style of family government. In summary, the benevolent style of family government is designed to promote the growth and welfare of the child in becoming all that God intends her or him to be. It takes into account both the inherent strengths and weaknesses of the child, and it also encourages children to develop their potential while dealing realistically with their sinful nature. It differs from authoritarianism in that it ascribes great value to each child and encourages the child to become increasingly autonomous; and it is unlike permissiveness in that it does not ignore or underestimate the power of sin and the necessity of parental direction and authority.

PARENTS
AS
PROVIDERS

Parental responsibilities can be broadly divided into providing, training, and correcting. In our definition here, providing refers to our responsibility to fulfill all of the needs of our children. Training refers to the process of parents guiding, instructing, and stimulating their children to develop moral, spiritual, intellectual, and social spheres of their lives. And correction refers to how we deal with our children's sinful or improper attitudes and behavior. In both God's dealings with us and in our dealings in our own families, children grow when there is ample provision followed by careful training and supplemented with discerning correction.

Although providing for the needs of children is the most obvious aspect of effective parenting, it is often seen too narrowly. We all know that an infant goes through a prolonged period of helplessness; everyone realizes that children could not live through their first years of life without adult care. Yet many parents fail to realize that the responsibility to provide for their children extends far beyond physical needs. In fact, after the first few months of life, providing for the emotional well-being of children is much more important than providing for their physical welfare.[1] And as children grow, their emotional and intellectual needs multiply while physical needs remain fairly constant and elementary.

Throughout Scripture God is revealed as our provider. There are countless verses that detail God's faithful provision for His children. In fact, some Bible scholars have shown that one of the names of God in Hebrew, El Shaddai, ties in closely with God's provision for His people. Nathan Stone commented:

> Shaddai itself occurs forty-eight times in the Old Testament and is translated "almighty." The other word so like it, and from which we believe it to be derived, occurs twenty-four times and is translated "breast." As connected with the word *breast* the title Shaddai signifies one who nourishes, supplies, satisfies. Connected with the word for God, El, it then becomes the "One mighty to nourish, satisfy, supply." Naturally, with God the idea would be intensified and it comes to mean the One who "sheds forth" and "pours out" sustenance and blessing. In this sense, then, God is the all-sufficient, the all-bountiful.[2]

The name El Shaddai is first used in the Bible in Genesis 17. God is speaking to Abram, who is ninety years old and "as good as dead" according to Hebrews 11:12, and He promises to provide him a son. God, the almighty provider, also promises to make him fruitful for generations to come, and we see the fulfillment of this promise today. Abraham's descendants cannot be numbered, and through them the whole world has been blessed.

Another example of God as provider occurs years later, when Isaac, the son of Abraham, sent his son Jacob to find a wife. Isaac appealed to "El Shaddai" when he spoke of Jacob being fruitful (Gen. 28:3). And when Jacob heard that his son Simeon was being held hostage in Egypt and that his beloved youngest son Benjamin might be the ransom, he looked to "El Shaddai" to save his children (Gen. 43:14).

Earthly parents are also instructed to provide for their children: "After all, children should not have to save up for their parents, but parents for their children" (2 Cor. 12:14).

As our children's suppliers, we often wonder what needs we are to fill. Paul provides an answer: "And my God will meet all your needs according to his glorious riches in Christ Jesus" (Phil. 4:19). The implication of this verse for parenting is clear: we are to supply all of our children's needs—physical needs, emotional needs, and spiritual needs.

Many Christian parents believe they have fulfilled their responsibility when they have provided for their children's physical and spiritual well-being. The sad fact is that many children from Christian homes rebel against their parents and God because they have unmet emotional needs. Children will thrive and mature only when provision for physical and spiritual needs takes place in an atmosphere that also encourages children to learn to express and understand their emotions.

Physical Needs

God's provision for Adam and Eve in the Garden of Eden was just the beginning of His care for the physical needs of His children. He provided food for Jacob and his family during seven years of famine by elevating Joseph to the position of second in command in Egypt (Gen. 41–48). And when the Israelites were living in the wilderness God miraculously provided both water (Exod. 17:1-7) and food (Exod. 16:11-18). His provision for Israel here was so complete that even their clothes and sandals did not wear out during their forty years of wandering (Deut. 29:5). And God's provision is not limited to Old Testament times.

Although he longed for privacy after being told of the beheading of John the Baptist, Christ fed more than 5,000 people who were following after him (Matt. 14:13-21). And on another occasion He assured His disciples: "If you, then, though you are evil, know how to give good gifts to your children, how much more will your Father in heaven give good gifts to those who ask Him!" (Matt. 7:11).

Within the human family also, parents are at all times providing for the physical well-being of their children. The infant at its mother's breast is totally dependent on another person for physical sustenance. As the child grows, this dependency gradually diminishes; but nonetheless throughout childhood and youth parents are legally and morally responsibile to provide for their children's physical needs.

The Need for Love

In creating Eve, God once and for all established a model that shows parents how to provide for the social needs of their children. Adam was the lone human on earth when God brought the animals to him to be named. The animals did provide a diversion for Adam, but of course social interaction was impossible. So God caused him to fall into a deep sleep, and He made Eve from one of Adam's ribs. When Adam awoke he said:

> "This is now bone of my bones,
> and flesh of my flesh;
> she shall be called 'woman,'
> for she was taken out of man."
> (Gen. 2:23)

Eve was created because it was "not good for the man to be alone" (Gen. 2:18). Adam needed a counterpart, a friend, a lover, and God gave him all of these in a wife. This marks the beginning of the family. Adam and Eve then fell into sin, and thus begins the long love story of God restoring His fallen creatures to communion with Him.

Maurice Wagner describes this love of God:

> We read, "He [the Father] hath made us accepted in the beloved [Christ]" (Eph. 1:6). We did absolutely nothing to earn that acceptance; we submitted to Him, and He made us accepted to Himself! . . .
> This great truth reinforces our sense of belongingness; indeed, it validates it. We are loved by God the Father with an unconditional, voluntary love. We know we belong to Him because of His immutable promises.[3]

As we read through Scripture we discover very significant insights into the ideal nature of love—God's love and parents' love. Love is, of course, unconditional (Rom. 5:8). It is eternal

(Jer. 31:3). It is self-sacrificing (1 Cor. 13:5; John 15:13). And it is patient (1 Cor. 13:4). Parental love partakes of these characteristics. And one of the most important aspects of parental love is this: It is expressed in actions so that the child can clearly comprehend it.

Most of us love our children, but often we become so entangled in the affairs of daily life that we fail to communicate our love in ways that our children can understand and accept. Often the father comes home from work too weary to enjoy the children. And most mothers, even if they are not working outside the home, spend only a small amount of time playing and sharing with their children.

Christ took time in the middle of a busy teaching ministry that was stirring increasing opposition to attend to little children (Matt. 19:13-14). And in the ultimate expression of love Jesus gave His life on the cross. His supreme sacrifice stands as our example for expressing love in visible and concrete ways.

With God as our model, we can understand why it is that love without corresponding actions cannot fulfill the deep needs of children. We must take time to demonstrate our love; we must look carefully at our priorities and perhaps eliminate some otherwise worthy activities that deprive our children of the loving companionship that is so essential to their growth.

The Need for Security

All children need a deep sense of security if they are to grow up with a positive attitude toward themselves and others. Here too God is the model for parents throughout Scripture. For example, He repeatedly delivers His children from danger. The rescue of Noah and his family from the flood (Gen. 6–8) and the protection of both Daniel (Dan. 6) and his friends (Dan. 3) were supernatural provisions for physical safety. In the New Testament we see Christ smothering a storm to calm the fears of His disciples (Matt. 8:23-27).

Scripture also speaks of emotional security—an inner peace

emanating from being loved by Christ and loving Him in turn. Christ tells the Pharisees: "My sheep listen to my voice; I know them, and they follow me. I give them eternal life, and they shall never perish; no one can snatch them out of my hand" (John 10:26-28). And the believer knows that, with the psalmist, he can confess to God: "Your hand will guide me, your right hand will hold me fast" (Ps. 139:10).

In Ephesians Paul tells believers they have been chosen by God (1:4), predestined to be sons (1:5), made acceptable to God (1:6), redeemed (1:7), forgiven (1:7), given an inheritance (1:11), and sealed with the Holy Spirit (1:13). This father-and-child relationship between the sovereign God of the universe and His creatures gives us impregnable security.

Parents who know their heavenly Father intimately will want to provide similar security for their children. An overprotective or overindulgent environment robs children of a sense of security. Our children need to know that no matter where they go they cannot remove themselves from our love. They need to know we will not turn on them in anger. They need to know we will stand by them and support them. They need to know that their father and mother are deeply committed to family harmony and unity. The parents will not break up the family and thereby deprive them of the security of family love and unity. And in the case of a broken marriage, children need to know that both parents still love them and that parental conflict will not deprive them of a loving relationship with each parent.

The Need for Confidence

Every child also has a strong need for confidence and inner strength. While security depends largely on our safety and the consistency of our external environment, confidence rests more on our sense of competence. It grows through personal accomplishments, new experiences, and the confidence that others have in us.

Here too God shows parents the way to build confidence in their children. Confidence is possible because He has endowed us with certain abilities, and, for the Christian, because of the presence of the indwelling Holy Spirit. We have all been created in God's image, and every person has capabilities and potential that God expects us to develop. Paul encouraged Timothy to develop his special talent—faithfulness—in these words: "Do not neglect your gift" (1 Tim. 4:14). Paul also described the power of God in the believer by saying, "I can do everything through him who gives me strength" (Phil. 4:13).

Another example from Scripture is Moses, who at one time was crippled by a lack of confidence. He had received the best in education because he was trained in the courts of Pharaoh after being adopted by the monarch's daughter. But he was a fugitive from justice when God came to commission him; so he asked God, "Who am I, that I should go to Pharaoh and should bring the Israelites out of Egypt?" (Exod. 3:11). God did not turn away from Moses for expressing anxiety and lack of confidence; He replied, "I will be with you" (Exod. 3:12). If we are to understand the force of this reassurance, we must look back to verse 6 where God had reminded him: "I am the God of your father, the God of Abraham, the God of Isaac and the God of Jacob."

But Moses' lack of confidence was overwhelming. He complained that the people of Israel would not listen to him (4:1); so God turned his staff into a snake as a sign of support (4:2-5). Then God turned Moses' hand leprous and returned it to health (4:6-9). Still Moses doubted. He objected that he was not eloquent (4:10), whereupon the Lord replied: "Who gave man his mouth? Who makes him deaf or dumb? Who gives him sight or makes him blind? Is it not I, the LORD? Now go; I will help you speak and will teach you what to say" (Exod. 4:11-12). When Moses still hung back, God appointed Aaron as his spokesman. Moses finally obeyed, and he went on to become the renowned deliverer of Israel.

Today, the encouragement and support of the Holy Spirit is a major source of confidence for believers. In the New Testament the Holy Spirit is described as a comforter, counselor, and encourager. And in the family, children need the support and encouragement of their parents if they are going to learn to face the difficulties of life with confidence. Many people suffer a lifetime of inadequacy and inferiority because their parents did not help them to develop security and confidence. The parents ridiculed their anxiety instead of soothing their fears, heaped up criticism instead of commending small accomplishments, and tore them down rather than sensitively providing for their vital needs. All children are gifted, but such an endowment is fragile. Children need loving care and wise direction from their parents. Just as our Father in heaven provides perfectly for us, we too should care for the children He has entrusted to us.

—6—

PARENTS
AS
TRAINERS

Disciplining children is another topic that is greatly misunderstood. Mention "discipline" to parents or children and they immediately think of punishment for misbehavior. This is a natural response, but one that is not supported by Scripture. There are two errors in this definition.

First, the idea that discipline is something parents do after a child misbehaves is incorrect. The second error is the assumption that discipline is the same as punishment. In the next three chapters we will attempt to put the concept of discipline in biblical perspective and show that there are two major responsibilities in discipline. One is the training function. The other is correction. We will see that both of these need to be distinguished from the biblical concept of punishment and that God's attitude of grace toward His children provides the framework for effective discipline.

Punishment and Discipline

Ask any Christian parent if God, as heavenly Father, punishes His children, and you are likely to hear a hearty yes. It is obvious, this person will assert, that God punishes His children. And they assume that they should do the same. But this is not the case. Much confusion and harm have resulted from the failure to differentiate between the concepts of punishment and discipline as they are presented in the Bible. Punishment is designed to satisfy God's justice and to execute His judgment on sin; whereas discipline is designed to promote the growth and maturity of the person being disciplined. Punishment is God dealing with the sinner; discipline is God dealing with His children.[1] When Christ died He suffered the punishment for the sins of all humanity. We read concerning His death: "God presented him as a sacrifice of atonement, through faith in his blood. He did this to demonstrate his justice, because in his forbearance he had left the sins committed beforehand unpunished" (Rom. 3:25).

At the moment Jesus died, all of the sins of every believer were paid for—past, present, and future. There is no such thing as punishment for the believer. There is discipline, but this is an entirely different matter. Those who do not accept Christ's payment, of course, face an eternity of punishment.

A comparison of Scripture passages will reveal the distinct purpose, focus, and attitude within both discipline and punishment. To begin with, the purpose of punishment is to vindicate God's holiness by inflicting a just penalty on the non-Christian. This is clearly stated in 2 Thess. 1:6-9:[2]

> God is just: He will pay back trouble to those who trouble you and give relief to you who are troubled, and to us as well. This will happen when the Lord Jesus is revealed from heaven in blazing fire with his powerful angels. He will punish those who do not know God and do not obey the gospel of our Lord Jesus. They will be punished with everlasting destruction and shut out from the presence of the Lord and from the majesty of his power.

The purpose of discipline, on the other hand, is to promote Christ-like attitudes and behavior in the child of God. We read in Hebrews: "Our fathers disciplined us for a little time as they thought best; but God disciplines us for our good, that we may share in His holiness" (Heb. 12:10).

Proverbs 29:15 points toward a second distinction between

discipline and punishment. "The rod of correction imparts wisdom, but a child left to itself disgraces his mother." We see here that in discipline the focus is on the future; in punishment, the focus is on the past. Discipline seeks to promote future Christ-like attitudes and behavior; punishment seeks to satisfy God's justice, which has been violated.

The third distinction between discipline and punishment is the attitude of the person in authority. Consider the following two Scripture passages: the first speaking of God's righteous punishment of the sinner and the second referring to His correction of His children.

> See, the day of the LORD is coming
> —a cruel day, with wrath and fierce anger—
> to make the land desolate
> and destroy the sinners within it. . . .
> I will punish the world for its evil,
> the wicked for their sins. . . .
> (Isa. 13:9, 11)

> My son, do not despise the LORD's discipline
> and do not resent his rebuke,
> because the LORD disciplines those he loves,
> as a father the son he delights in.
> (Prov. 3:11-12)

Here we have a great contrast. God's attitude in punishing sinners is righteous anger; His attitude in disciplining His children is loving correction. A table summarizes the three distinctions discussed above.

	PUNISHMENT	DISCIPLINE
PURPOSE	To satisfy the demands of justice	To promote growth and maturity
FOCUS	Sinful deeds and attitudes of the past	Christ-like deeds and attitudes in the future
ATTITUDE	Anger	Love

At the heart of these distinctions is the difference between a righteous judge and a loving father. In meting out punishment, or judgment, to the unsaved, God is revealing His holiness. Once a sinner's account is settled, however, God responds only as a loving Father. His correction is designed to produce righteousness in His children, not to inflict a penalty.

These three distinctions establish a fundamental principle for the Christian parent. If we follow God's pattern we will never respond to our children in order to "get even," to release hostile feelings, or even to satisfy God's justice. Instead we will apply Romans 12:19 and Deut. 32:35—" 'It is mine to avenge, I will repay,' says the Lord"—to our relations with our children. And we will not see it as our responsibility to inflict punishment. Instead, we will lovingly, yet with firmness and consistency, correct them with a view to generating Christ-like attitudes and actions in the future.

This does not mean that we must eliminate traditional forms of discipline. For example, spanking children or sending them to their room can be either discipline or punishment. If our children misbehave and we spank them or send them to their room in anger, we are punishing. Our attitude here is anger, our purpose is retribution, and our focus is past action. But if our children misbehave and we are motivated by love to spank them or to have them spend a few minutes in their room to learn to be more thoughtful next time, we are disciplining.

Many times, unfortunately, we rationalize that punishment is for our child's own good. Even when we are extremely angry, we tell ourselves, *"She deserved it!" "It's what she needs!"* or *"It's for his own good!"* We wrongly conclude that since our child misbehaved, our intervention must have been constructive discipline. But if we look to God's pattern revealed in Scripture we will have to acknowledge that responding to our children in anger is not discipline but punishment. God never disciplines in anger since His wrath for the sins of His children was settled at the cross (Rom. 5:9, 8:1; Gal. 3:13; 1 Peter 3:18).

One way for us to determine whether we are punishing or disciplining is to look at our motivation. Are we acting out of a strong commitment to our child's growth, or are we trying to cause the child to "shape up" in order to get rid of our own frustration? If we are honest with ourselves, I think we will find that we often "correct" our children in order to relieve our own irritation rather than to promote the child's benefit.

Another way to gauge whether we are punishing or disciplining is to note the child's reaction. Punishment brings fear, hostility, and guilt. Discipline brings security and respect.

The best example of the absence of fear is found in 1 John 4:18: "There is no fear in love. But perfect love drives out fear, because fear has to do with punishment. The man who fears is not made perfect in love." Here we are told that the fear of punishment has already been taken care of for the child of God.[3] That is why believers can have confidence when they look ahead to the day of judgment. This security in Jesus Christ is a model for our relationships with our children.

Angry punishment breeds fear in children, but loving correction generates security. This does not mean that children will always look forward to correction or that some discipline is not painful or unpleasant. The Book of Hebrews tells us that "no discipline seems pleasant at the time" (12:11), but discipline administered in love does promote a sense of security and belonging in the child and produces fruits of righteousness. An example of such fruit is the child who obeys her or his parents out of love—love for the parents and love for God's moral precepts.

The difference between punishment and discipline is fundamental to child rearing. It provides a foundation for interaction with our children. As God's appointed representatives, we have a responsibility to train and correct our children, but nowhere are we instructed to be agents of punishment.

Training

We are now ready to examine what the Bible has to say about training children. The most familiar promise to parents in the Bible is found in Proverbs 22:6: "Train a child in the way he should go, and when he is old he will not turn from it." The word *khanakh,* here translated "train," is especially pertinent to our study of child training. *Khanakh* or its root is also used in Genesis 14:14; Deuteronomy 20:5; and 1 Kings 8:63.

In Genesis 14 *khanakh* is translated "trained," and it refers to the 318 experienced and trusted men Abraham summoned to rescue his nephew Lot, who was being held captive. In Deuteronomy 20 the word is translated "dedicated," and it refers to the religious ceremonies that attended taking possession of a new home in Israel. Again in 1 Kings 8:63 it is translated "dedicated," and the context here is the dedication of the magnificent temple in Jerusalem by Solomon and the nation of Israel.

So *khanakh* refers to training in a very broad sense. Nowhere in Scripture is it used to imply correction for wrongdoing. It applies to the total process of educating, instructing, and developing maturity and character within children. Training, the subject of the remainder of this chapter, is one of the two functions of "discipline." The second function, correction, will be treated in chapter 7.

Proverbs 22:6 is frequently used to teach that children should be shaped and directed into a certain Christian pattern in order to ensure their later faithfulness to Christian beliefs. Well-meaning but misinformed parents and religious leaders have believed that this verse exhorts parents to mold their children into a special form of Christian character. Unfortunately, this misses the biblical intent.

Charles Swindoll sardonically paraphrases this interpretation of Proverbs 22:6 as follows:

> Be sure your child is in Sunday school and church regularly. Cement into his mind a few memory verses from the Bible, plus some hymns and prayers. Send him to Christian camps during the summers of his formative years, and certainly, if at all possible, place the child in a Christian school so he can be educated by people whose teaching is based on the Bible. Because, after all, someday he will sow his wild oats. For sure, he will have his

fling. But when he gets old enough to get over his fling he will come back to God.[4]

This caricature makes an important point. There are indeed many people who misunderstand the phrase "in the way." Most of us believe that "the way" refers to an external standard to which children should conform or some direction imposed on them by an outside authority.

However, most theologians agree with the interpretation offered by J. P. Lange: " 'The way' can have no other meaning than 'according to the standard of his way.' . . . in the sense of his own natural and characteristic style and manner,'—and then his training will have reference to that to which he is naturally fitted."[5] In other words, parents are to train their children so that they will develop fully and become the unique beings God has destined them to be. This, of course, is a very different matter than shaping a child according to an established religious mold.

Another passage in Proverbs has rich implications for the phrase "in the way." The writer exclaims:

> There are three things that are too amazing for me,
>   four which I do not understand:
> the way of an eagle in the sky,
>   the way of a snake on a rock,
> the way of a ship on the high seas,
>   and the way of a man with a maiden.
>   (Prov. 30:18-19)

Three examples from nature and one from human relations are used to describe the wondrous complexity of everything God has created. The way of an eagle, a snake, and a ship and the way of a man with a young woman are never narrow or closely defined. Instead, each is the unfolding and blossoming of innate qualities and characteristics. Each is a mystery that captures the awe and respect of the observer. Everything created by God has a beauty and a uniqueness that is beyond understanding. The wonder of a man and woman in love suggests the rich gifts and boundless potential that God has given to every human being, including children.

This is the long-range view of Proverbs 22:6. And far from instructing us to lay out the course of our children's lives, this passage exhorts us to be sensitive to each child's individual attributes, manners, and style. Parents who follow the biblical model of training become sensitive to their child's "way" and, within that context, train the child into full maturity.

Another biblical concept closely related to the "training" in Proverbs 22:6 is embodied in the Greek noun *paideia* and its verb form *paideuō.*[6] The noun form is translated "training" (Eph. 6:4; 2 Tim. 3:16) and "discipline" (Heb. 12:5, 7, 8, 11). The verb is translated "punish" (Luke 23:16, 22), "educate" (Acts 7:22), "train" (Acts 22:3), "discipline" (1 Cor. 11:32; Heb. 12:6, 7, 10; Rev. 3:19), "beat" (2 Cor. 6:9), "teach" (1 Tim. 1:20; Titus 2:12), and "instruct" (2 Tim. 2:25). This wide range of meanings shows that *paideia* refers to the whole process of disciplining children. It includes correction for wrongdoing as well as training.

In Acts 7:22, for example, we are told that Moses was "educated in all the wisdom of the Egyptians." And in Acts 22:3 Paul says he was "thoroughly trained in the law of our fathers." Both of these passages refer to education rather than correction. Moses was educated in the major learning center of his day and Paul listened at the feet of the scholar Gamaliel. In Titus 2:12 Paul tells us that the grace of God "teaches" us. And in 2 Timothy 3:16 he says that all Scripture is useful for "training" in righteousness. All of these verses refer to the educational aspect of discipline.

In the Book of Hebrews we find one of several instances in which *paideia* refers to correction. This correction is what most parents think of when they hear the word *discipline.* The writer of Hebrews points the reader to an Old Testament passage—Proverbs 3:11-12—that addresses believers as children of God: "My son, do not regard lightly the discipline of the LORD, nor faint when you are reproved by Him; for those whom the LORD loves He disciplines, and He scourges every son whom He receives" (Heb. 12:5-6 NASB). Here is an obvious reference to correction—that is, responding to misdeeds.

We read that the child of God is both corrected ("scourges") and "disciplined."

Taken together, these uses of the terms *paideia* and *khanakh* discredit the notion that disciplining children consists of correction alone. Rather, they demonstrate the breadth of the biblical concept of discipline.

In the next chapter we will look further at Old Testament concepts of discipline. For now we simply want to note that discipline is not only, nor even primarily, the corrective measures a parent takes when a child has misbehaved. Discipline is the total process of both training and correcting children. This is what Ephesians 6:4 refers to when it tells fathers to bring up their children "in the training [KJV, "*nurture*"] and instruction of the Lord."

Instruction

An important part of our training function is instruction. In Deuteronomy 6:1-9 we have a beautiful description of positive parenting. The children of Israel were to *do* the commandments of God (vv. 1-3). They were to *love* God (vv. 4-5). And they were to *place* His words in their heart (v. 6). Then, and only then, were they to *teach* them to their children (vv. 7-9). The parents' walk with God was first to be personal and experiential. They were to be examples; then they were to instruct.

The nature of this instruction deserves our special consideration. Many parents are looking to their church, their Christian school, their mealtime prayers, or their family devotions for their children's spiritual training. But according to this passage of Scripture spiritual instruction was to be a way of living. It was to be carried out (1) when they sat at home, (2) when they walked along the road, (3) when they lay down, and (4) when they rose up. In other words, spiritual instruction was to be an ongoing practice that would become a natural part of family life. It was not to be relegated to morning or evening prayers nor consigned to teachers—even Christian ones!

A few years ago my son and I were working in the garden. "Did God make weeds, Daddy?" Dickie asked, puzzled.

I started to give a quick answer so that I could go on with my work, but then I realized that this was an opportunity to teach a spiritual lesson.

I laid down my weeding fork and said, "Dickie, you know about Adam and Eve. They were the first people who ever lived on earth. God put them in a beautiful garden without *any* weeds. Then one day the devil came along, and he looked like a snake. He told Adam and Eve to disobey God; he said they should eat some fruit God had told them not to eat. And you know what happened? They ate it. Then the world started having problems. After Adam and Eve disobeyed God, weeds started growing and they had to go to work and leave their pretty garden."

With a serious look Dickie replied, "Isn't that a shame!"

I relate this incident to illustrate an important biblical principle: Lessons arising out of real-life experiences are usually much more effective than formal learning.

This real-life instruction is what is spoken of in Deuteronomy 6. The Israelites were to weave child training into the fabric of their daily lives. In our culture we have a strong tendency to separate the sacred and the secular. We see to it that our children receive education (at school), training (at home), and spiritual instruction (at church, at family devotions, and, in some cases, at school).

But this compartmentalizing creates problems. One of the reasons so many children and young adults from Christian homes find little meaning in their Christian experience is that their Christian faith was never integrated with daily living. Their parents failed to experience or failed to convey their joy at God's creative genius shown in nature. They failed to see and explain their business and family affairs from God's perspective—His children gaining dominion over the world for the glory of their Creator. As a result, their children failed to see that God is deeply interested and involved in every area of life.

Salvation

Scripture places a strong burden of responsibility on parents for the salvation of their children. For example, the people of Israel were commanded to tell their children repeatedly of their deliverance from bondage in Egypt (Deut. 6:20-25). Can you imagine the awe the Israelite children must have experienced when their parents and grandparents told them of the spectacular plagues God launched against Pharaoh, the miraculous crossing of the Red Sea, and bread coming from heaven? Although we cannot recount such dramatic incidents today, every Christian parent has experienced spiritual deliverance that changed the course of her or his life. For some there may have been a profound release from guilt and an assurance of salvation, while for others perhaps it was the spiritual growth and vitality that resulted from living in a family that was regularly experiencing God's deliverance. Whatever our Christian experience may have been, we should encourage our children to develop and expand their commitment to God.

Noah's family escaped the flood because their father was righteous (Gen. 7:1). And when Paul and Silas told the Philippian jailer that if he would believe on Jesus he would be saved, they included the words, "and your household" (Acts 16:31). What follows is a moving account of a family's first experience of new life in Christ.

> At that hour of the night the jailer took them and washed their wounds; then immediately he and all his family were baptized. The jailer brought them into his house and set a meal before them, and the whole family was filled with joy, because they had come to believe in God. (Acts 16:33-34)

As we recount God's dealing in our lives, it is natural for children to want to follow our example and place their trust in God. And what a deep joy it is for us to be able to respond to this interest in salvation and point out how our children too can become members of God's family.

We will now look at four other aspects that Scripture includes within child training. There are many others, but these are certainly key ingredients in effective child rearing.

Obedience

Abraham, the father of the Jewish nation, is known as a man of faith. But Scripture also reveals that God chose Abraham "so that he will direct his children and his household after him to keep the way of the LORD by doing what is right and just" (Gen. 18:19). He knew that Abraham could teach his children obedience.

Surely this is an important aspect of child training. If our children are going to learn to follow God's guidance and the leadership of others in authority, they must first learn to follow our instruction. In another Old Testament passage we read: "My son, keep your father's commands and do not forsake your mother's teaching" (Prov. 6:20). In the New Testament Paul writes, "Children, obey your parents in the Lord, for this is right" (Eph. 6:1). And in describing the qualities that should mark an officer of the church, Paul states: "He must manage his own family well and see that his children obey him with proper respect" (1 Tim. 3:4).

As we saw in chapter 4, we need to avoid the extremes of both permissiveness and authoritarianism. We must not fail to teach our children to obey, but we must also avoid creating the slavish conformity that is the result of fear and pressure. God does not force us to do His bidding. He loves us, counsels us in His Word, and sets the perfect example. And He tells us that if we love Him we will keep His commands (1 John 5:1-3). So too in parenting, love and consistent training—not power, pressure, nagging, and coercion—are the keys to teaching our children to obey.

Relationships

The Bible puts a high priority on our relationships with others. We read concerning friendship: "A friend loves at all times, and a brother is born for adversity" (Prov. 17:17).

When he describes what it is to live as children of the light, Paul points us to love: "Be imitators of God, therefore, as dearly loved children and live a life of love, just as Christ loved us and gave himself up for us as a fragrant offering and sacrifice to God" (Eph. 5:1-2). One of the major tasks of parents is to help their children learn to enjoy and appreciate other people and to interact with them in love. Children are prone to be envious, jealous, fearful, and argumentative. They are also easily influenced by their friends. So they need parents who set a positive example, who help them handle conflicts calmly, and who are interested in their friends—thereby demonstrating the value they place on relationships. In short, children need our sensitive help in developing social skills that will serve them throughout life.

Prayer

In Philippians 4:6, as well as in other Scripture passages, we are encouraged to pray in every circumstance: "Do not be anxious about anything, but in everything, by prayer and petition, with thanksgiving, present your requests to God." Parents who want their children to develop a vital relationship with God should make prayer a meaningful family experience. We need to avoid elaborate, irrelevant prayers and concentrate instead on thanking God for providing so bountifully and petitioning Him for daily needs and opportunities.

Many families find that maintaining a prayer list and a record of answers to prayer confirms that God is powerful and that He does care for us. And many families have discovered that when every member, children included, knows the persons in a missionary family, then the family begins to pray earnestly together. First-hand reports from the missionary family, such as letters and home visits, become stimulating experiences that each person and the family as a whole can share. Conversational prayer has transformed many a family prayer time from the monotony of routine to the profound experience of the grace of God.[7] This style of prayer, which emphasizes short, personal communication with God, can open new vistas in a child's experience of the presence of God.

Love

The most important aspect of training children is training them to love. Christ said, "All men will know that you are my disciples if you love one another" (John 13:35). Love is both the source and the wellspring of obedience, prayer, and lasting relationships with others. It is also the source of our confidence and security.

We should remember that if children are not able to love, virtues such as obedience, and many others not mentioned here, will take on a false or superficial taint. Conformity unaccompanied by love is not obedience. It is simply giving in to fear. And prayer without love is not communion with God. It is simply another habit or routine.

Since we will deal in great depth with the significance of our children's love, we will simply mark three truisms here. First, love is the most important virtue we can help our children develop. And second, love is better caught than taught—that is, love is the child's response to loving, giving, and forgiving parents. And, third, it is not enough to love our children. We must not be satisfied until we have learned to communicate our love in such a way that our children understand it and receive it.

Summary

Training refers to all of the instruction and guidance that parents offer their children. These actions, coupled with their loving provision and setting a Christian example, enable children to grow up in their way—that is, according to the unique unfolding and complete fulfillment of their God-given capabilities.

—7—

ΦARENTS AS CORRECTORS

Having looked at our role in providing and training, we now turn to our responsibility to correct our children. We should keep in mind that the order in these tasks of parenthood is modeled on God's dealings with us as His children: first comes the provision; next comes training and instruction; and last comes correction.

When God placed Adam and Eve in the Garden he first provided for their needs. Then He instructed them in their responsibilities: be fruitful, fill the earth and subdue it, rule over every living creature—but bypass the tree of knowledge of good and evil. Afterward, God corrected. All correction should have its roots planted firmly in the soil of parental provision and training. Without these preparatory steps, correction lacks continuity and purpose.

Consider, for example, two children at home with very little to do. Father is at work and mother is busy with household tasks. They have not planned any activities for the children to do, and by midmorning the children are bored.

"What can we do?" they plead.

"Why don't you go out and play?" mother replies offhandedly, as she goes about her work.

The children disappear but soon return with the same question. This time mother makes another suggestion or two that again have little appeal for the children. Soon both mother and children are exasperated. The children are still arguing and scrapping when mother interrupts her work to banish them to their room with the threat that something severe will result if they don't mend their ways.

These children are not "bad" or intent on stirring up trouble. And they weren't being disobedient. They were simply bored because their parents hadn't taken time to be sure there were some stimulating things for them to do.

If the parents had done this, unnecessary hassles, hurt feelings, and frayed nerves would have been avoided. And the time invested in helping the children begin these activities would be less than the total time spent in correction.

This principle applies equally to relating to teen-agers. Many of us do not take time to talk with our teen-agers, attend their school events, or share enjoyable times with them. When the neglected daughter or son turns to questionable activities and friends we wonder why. Often the reason is that we have failed to show our teen-ager how to enjoy life through family fun and wholesome friendships outside the family.

Old Testament Concepts of Discipline

In chapter 6 we saw that the word *paideia* encompasses both a broad training function and a correction function. Two Hebrew words help us understand varied modes and effects of discipline. The first is *yasar.*

The Scriptures portray two aspects of *yasar:* the first is training or instruction—usually by words; the second refers to chastening, or physical correction. Following are examples of the instructive aspect.

> From heaven he made you hear his voice to discipline you. On earth he showed you his great fire, and you heard his words from out of the fire. (Deut. 4:36)

> I will praise the LORD, who counsels me;
> even at night my heart instructs me.
> (Ps. 16:7)

> I trained them and strengthened them,
>   but they plot evil against me.
>   (Hos. 7:15)

Yasar, then, is used to refer to training or instruction in various contexts. In one case the voice of the Lord is said to "discipline." Instruction also comes from the heart. In the last reference *yasar* refers to arming or training for war.

The second use of *yasar* is illustrated in the life of Rehoboam, shortly after he became king of Israel. Asked to lighten the tremendous burden his father had put on the people, Rehoboam rejected the plea. He said:

> "My father made your yoke heavy; I will make it even heavier. My father scourged you with whips; I will scourge you with scorpions." (1 Kings 12:14)

Here, as in the proverb below, *yasar* is used in the corrective sense, with physical discipline suggested.

> Discipline your son, and he will give you peace
>   he will bring delight to your soul.
>   (Prov. 29:17)

Discipline involves not only training and instruction, it also includes correction following misdeeds.

The other Hebrew word shedding light on the biblical concept of child training is *musar*. Generally translated "discipline," it typically communicates something you listen to—that is, words, and acts that follow those words.[1] Consider the following usages:

> Do not withhold discipline from a child;
>   if you punish him with the rod, he will not die.
>   (Prov. 23:13)

> Buy the truth and do not sell it;
>   get wisdom, discipline and understanding.
>   (Prov. 23:23)

> I went past the field of the sluggard,
>   past the vineyard of the man who lacks judgment;
> thorns had come up everywhere,

the ground was covered with weeds,
and the stone wall was in ruins.
I applied my heart to what I observed
and *learned a lesson* from what I saw. (Italics mine)
(Prov. 24:30-32)

In one passage instruction comes through physical pain; in another *musar* (here translated "discipline") is put alongside wisdom and understanding; in the third instruction comes through contemplation.

The use of *yasar* and *musar* in the Old Testament reflects the breadth of the biblical concept of discipline. According to the Bible, discipline is not simply the actions a parent takes after a child misbehaves, and it certainly is not limited to physical correction. It involves training, communication, circumstances, reflection and understanding.

The parable of the lost son is an excellent example of a parent choosing not to intervene in a child's sinful ways. Here the child learns from the consequences of misdeeds. In this story correction issues out of circumstances that are the natural result of the son's misbehavior. We do not read that the father tried to prevent his son from leaving home, though he probably did advise him not to misuse his new resources.

The son played fast and loose with both his goods and his life, and he soon found himself without money or friends. To keep alive he took a job feeding swine—not a prestigious occupation, especially for a Jewish lad! On the verge of starvation he came to his senses and realized that his father's servants were better off than he. So he decided to return home and ask his father for work.

But the father saw his son while he was still far away, and he ran to him, threw his arms around him, and kissed him. There was no scolding ("I told you so!") or interrogation ("Where have you been?") or lecture ("You should have listened to me."). In fact, the father had welcomed him home before he had a chance to say he was sorry. He didn't need to be told the error of his way; he had learned a lesson that words could never convey. Correction had done its work.

Correction was the result of a process that included losing

an inheritance, the pain of starvation, and the ashes of riotous living. He was home and loved and sheltered, but his inheritance was gone—the natural consequence of sinful living.[2] His father did not re-parcel the estate and give him a portion of his brother's inheritance; he had to live with the consequences of his behavior.[3]

Principles of Correction

As was the case in our discussion of training in chapter 6, this survey of the biblical pattern of correction does not present techniques. Beyond citing the use of words, natural consequences, and the rod, we see little specific biblical advice on what to do when we correct. We are not told, for example, at what ages or for what misdeeds children should be spanked. We are not told whether sending a child to bed is appropriate. We are not instructed about curfews, groundings, or other responses that parents can use.

We conclude from this that beyond the techniques clearly laid out in Scripture (reproof, consequences, and the rod) basic principles are more important than specifics. In other words, God has laid out both a biblical pattern for parent-child relations and a number of clear principles. But He has not given us many techniques of correction, much less a proper response to every parenting problem. Techniques and responses will vary from age to age, from culture to culture, and from child to child. No strategy or remedy could fit all situations, but the underlying principles for dealing with human problems, including those of child rearing, do not change. Drawing upon the Scriptures discussed earlier, we can suggest nine principles of correction.

1. *Correction will be preceded by the parents' positive example.*

> These are the commands, decrees and laws the LORD your God directed me to teach you to observe in the land that you are crossing the Jordan to possess, so that you, your children and their children after them may fear the LORD your God. . . . (Deut. 6:1-2)

How easy it is to tell our children what to do—but how difficult it often is to live the way we want them to! This Scripture passage is the beginning of the biblical model of correction: parents are first to set the example.

2. *Correction will be preceded by parents providing for the child's physical, social, emotional, and spiritual needs.*

Which of you fathers, if your son asks for a fish, will give him a snake instead? Or if he asks for an egg, will give him a scorpion? If you then, though you are evil, know how to give good gifts to your children, how much more will your Father in heaven give the Holy Spirit to those who ask him! (Luke 11:11-13)

Unless we provide freely for our children's needs they will not love or respect us, and they will resist or reject our efforts to correct them.

3. *Correction will be preceded by instruction.*

Therefore, since we are surrounded by such a great cloud of witnesses, let us throw off everything that hinders and the sin that so easily entangles, and let us run with perseverance the race marked out for us. Let us fix our eyes on Jesus, the author and perfecter of our faith, who for the joy set before him endured the cross, scorning its shame, and sat down at the right hand of the throne of God. Consider him who endured such opposition from sinful men, so that you will not grow weary and lose heart. In your struggle against sin, you have not yet resisted to the point of shedding your blood. And you have forgotten that word of encouragement that addresses you as sons: "My son, do not make light of the Lord's discipline, and do not lose heart when he rebukes you." (Heb. 12:1-5)

Sometimes we correct our children for things they didn't realize were wrong. In this passage the author of Hebrews first instructs readers and challenges them to a certain style of life, and then reminds them that such sonship will include correction.

4. *Correction will be done in love, not out of frustration.*

"Those whom I love I rebuke and discipline. So be earnest, and repent." (Rev. 3:19)

Correction is part of discipline. And, as we have seen, genuine discipline is done in love; punishment flows from anger.

5. *Correction will be done for the welfare of the child.*

Endure hardship as discipline; God is treating you as sons. For what son is not disciplined by his father? If you are not disciplined (and everyone undergoes discipline), then you are illegitimate children and not true sons. (Heb. 12:7-8)

How readily we say, "I'm doing this for your own good!" when, in fact, our patience and self-control are gone and we have succumbed to irritation and anger.

6. *Correction will produce security and respect.*

My son, do not despise the LORD'S discipline
   and do not resent his rebuke,
because the LORD disciplines those he loves,
   as a father the son he delights in.
   (Prov. 3:11-12)

There is no fear in love. But perfect love drives out fear, because fear has to do with punishment. The man who fears is not made perfect in love. (1 John 4:18)

Biblical correction, done in love for the child's benefit, produces security and respect and promotes maturity. Punishment, motivated by anger and the desire for revenge, provokes fear and resentment.

7. *Correction will be prayerfully designed and carried out.*
Manoah and his wife, an Israelite couple who lived approximately halfway between Jerusalem and the land of the Philistines, were childless. Because Israel was sinful God allowed them to be oppressed by the Philistines for forty years.

One day the angel of the Lord came to the woman and told her she would give birth to a son who would help to deliver Israel from the tyranny of the Philistines. When Manoah heard this message, he immediately turned to the Lord for guidance: " 'O Lord, I beg you, let the man of God you sent to us come again to teach us how to bring up the boy who is to be born' " (Judg. 13:8).

God answered Manoah's prayer and the angel of the Lord appeared again to tell Manoah and his wife how to rear their child in preparation for his great task. This couple began their child rearing ackowledging their lack of expertise and seeking God's guidance. For us, as well as Samson's parents, prayer does not mean that we will avoid the hardships of rearing children, but it is a major pillar in the awesome task of nurturing our children.

8. *Correction will be fair and sensitive.*

Fathers, do not exasperate your children; instead, bring them up in the training and instruction of the Lord. (Eph. 6:4)

Fathers, do not embitter your children, or they will become discouraged. (Col. 3:21)

Our child's reaction to correction is a clue to its suitability and effectiveness. Biblical discipline, born of love and sensitivity, does not cause children to despair. Paul gives us a crucial principle for effective discipline.

9. *Correction will promote understanding and communication.* God's discipline does not leave us confused, resentful, or withdrawn. In Hebrews 12:11 we read that this discipline produces the "harvest of righteousness." In Galatians Paul lists the fruits of spiritual training—love, joy, peace, patience, kindness, goodness, faithfulness, gentleness, and self-control (Gal. 5:22-23). God's wise discipline produces a greater understanding of ourselves and of Him and leads to improved communication between us. Similarly, biblical correction of our children stimulates deeper understanding and rapport between ourselves and our children.

DISCIPLINE BY GRACE

According to Scripture, there are two ways for people to relate to God. Similarly, there are two ways for parents to relate to children. The first of these is by law. The second is by grace. In the great biblical truth of God's grace we have one of the most frequently overlooked yet central components of the biblical model of parent-child relations. In fact, all that we have said so far about child training and correction can be summed up in a proper understanding and channeling of the grace of God in the lives of parents.

It is grace that enables us to accept our children regardless of their behavior. It is grace that empowers us to correct a delinquent child in love. And it is grace that motivates us to forgive quickly and lead our child on to improved behavior. In contrast, law authorizes us to make demands on our children, pressure and coerce them, and focus on external standards—all of which evoke untold resentment and despair.

In writing to Titus, his "true son in our common faith" (Titus 1:4), the apostle Paul declares that the grace of God teaches us how to live—positively and negatively. "It teaches us to say 'No' to ungodliness and worldly passions, and to live self-controlled, upright and godly lives in this present age"

74

(Titus 2:12). The surprising thing about this statement is that the Greek verb here translated "teaches" (*paideuō*) is from the same root as the noun translated "discipline" in Hebrews 12:5-8 and "training" in Ephesians 6:4. In other words, Paul says that as God's children we are disciplined by grace. It is the grace of God that enlightens, trains, motivates, and fortifies us! All spiritual instruction, all admonition, all exhortation, and all divine reproof and correction are ingredients of God's discipline of grace.

Grace, concisely defined as "God's unmerited favor," encompasses God's dealings with sinful humanity. It includes God's forgiveness, His love, His offer of salvation, and His provision for His children as a loving Father rather than as righteous judge. To understand how the scriptural concept of God's grace is applicable to parent-child relations we need first to outline the essential aspects of the biblical concepts of law and grace.

Contrasts Between Law and Grace

Nearly every Christian has some familiarity with the nature of law and grace. If nothing more, Christians recognize that their salvation is a gift of God and therefore an aspect of His grace (Eph. 2:8-9). Many Christians fail to understand, however, that God's law is much more than "the law of Moses" and that grace extends far beyond salvation. Law and grace in their pure forms are actually two systems of relating, each with its own set of governing principles. Law, the more evident system in Old Testament times, was preparatory to the principles of grace revealed through Christ. Outwardly, law and grace may produce similar results; inwardly, however, they are diametrically opposed.[1]

This is why the Bible teaches that law and grace are not compatible. Consider, for example, the following passages:

> Before this faith came, we were held prisoners by the law, locked up until faith should be revealed. So the law was put in charge to lead us to Christ that we might be justified by faith. Now that faith has come, we are no longer under the supervision of the law. (Gal. 3:23-25)

> Christ is the end of the law so that there may be right-
> eousness for everyone who believes. (Rom. 10:4)

To grasp more fully the contrast between law and grace and
to draw applications for parent-child relations, we will look at
five principles that characterize relationships based on law
and five principles of grace.

The first and perhaps the most basic principle of law is that
acceptance is based on one's performance. Acceptance, in
other words, is conditional. It is earned *through* our actions or
works. In contrast, under grace, acceptance is unconditional.
Grace reverses the principle of law. Under grace, performance flows *from* acceptance. It is a voluntary response to the
fact that we have been accepted. Paul wrote:

> In love he predestined us to be adopted as his sons
> through Jesus Christ, in accordance with his pleasure
> and will—to the praise of his glorious grace, which he
> has freely given us in the One he loves. In him we have
> redemption through his blood, the forgiveness of sins, in
> accordance with the riches of God's grace that he
> lavished on us with all wisdom and understanding. (Eph.
> 1:4b-8)

The child of God does not work to gain acceptance. In fact,
there is not one thing we can do to make ourselves one bit
more acceptable to God—because all efforts would fall short
of the perfection required. We are made totally acceptable to
God at the moment we place our trust in Christ as Savior.

A second distinction between law and grace is this: under
law, blessings are earned; under grace, blessings are un-
earned. In Deuteronomy 28 Moses is presenting part of Israel's law system, and this passage also portrays the concept of
earned blessings. He begins by saying: "If you fully obey the
LORD your God and carefully follow all his commands I give
you today, the LORD your God will set you high above all the
nations of the earth" (v. 1). The verses that follow list a wide
range of blessings for Israel *if* they kept God's commandments. So blessings were conditional under the law system of
the Old Testament.

In contrast, Paul writes:

> Praise be to the God and Father of our Lord Jesus
> Christ, who has blessed us in the heavenly realms with
> every spiritual blessing in Christ. For he chose us in him
> before the creation of the world to be holy and blameless
> in his sight. (Eph. 1:3-4)

We have already been given all spiritual blessings. There is
nothing more for us to earn. Under grace, blessings are freely
given, apart from works. Chafer puts it well:

> The basic principle of grace is the fact that *all* blessings
> originate with God, and are offered to man *graciously.*
> The formula of grace is, "I have blessed you, therefore
> be good." Thus it is revealed that the motive for right
> conduct under grace is not to secure the favor of God,
> which already exists toward saved and unsaved to an
> infinite degree through Christ; it is rather a matter of
> consistent action in view of such divine grace.[2]

Closely related to the necessity to earn blessings is the third
principle of the law system: Under law, punishment and
curses follow unacceptable performance; under grace,
punishment and curses have no place. In the same chapter
that the rich blessings for obedience are recorded Moses also
spells out an equally wide range of curses that would attend
Israel's disobedience (Deut. 28:15-68). If Israel did keep
God's commands He would bless them. If they did not they
would be punished.

In great contrast to this principle, Paul tells us: "Therefore,
there is now no condemnation for those who are in Christ
Jesus" (Rom. 8:1). And Peter elaborates on this concept: "He
[Christ] himself bore our sins in his body on the tree, so that
we might die to sins and live for righteousness; by his wounds
you have been healed" (1 Peter 2:24). When Christ died on
the cross He received all of the punishment we deserve. Because of that God no longer deals with us in punishment and
anger but solely in a discipline of grace. There is discipline in
the life of God's children—but not one bit of punishment.

Another contrast between law and grace has to do with the

focus of attention. Under law, actions are in focus. Under grace, internal attitudes and motives are in focus. This is the difference between the letter and the spirit of law. The Pharisees of Christ's day were sticklers for external details. They had hundreds of standards to guide daily conduct, including rules about diet and a complex set of laws concerning the Sabbath. But Jesus called the Pharisees whitened sepulchres for their hypocrisy.

When they criticized His disciples for picking grain on the Sabbath, Jesus turned this around by saying: "The Son of Man is Lord of the Sabbath" (Matt. 12:8). When they dismissed the healing of the blind and mute man possessed by a demon as the work of the devil, Jesus explained their preoccupation with faultfinding: "You brood of vipers, how can you who are evil say anything good? For out of the overflow of the heart the mouth speaks" (Matt. 12:34). So the New Testament standards of grace, which are far higher than the law, relate to internal qualities.

The fifth contrast between law and grace is that under law, fear is a prime motivator; under grace, love is the motivator. The Book of Hebrews points to the difference between Old Testament Israel's experience of God and the New Testament believer's relationship with God:

> You have not come to a mountain that can be touched and that is burning with fire; to darkness, gloom and storm; to a trumpet blast or to such a voice speaking words, so that those who heard it begged that no further word be spoken to them, because they could not bear what was commanded: "If even an animal touches the mountain, it must be stoned." The sight was so terrifying that Moses said, "I am trembling with fear." But you have come to Mount Zion, to the heavenly Jerusalem, the city of the living God. You have come to thousands upon thousands of angels in joyful assembly, to the church of the firstborn, whose names are written in heaven. You have come to God, the judge of all men, to the spirits of righteous men made perfect, to Jesus the mediator of a new covenant, and to the sprinkled blood that speaks a better word than the blood of Abel. (Heb. 12:18-24)

And Paul shows that love fulfills the law: "The entire law is summed up in a single command: 'Love your neighbor as yourself' " (Gal. 5:14).
In the law system predominant in the Old Testament fear was an important ingredient. God's requirements were stated and His judgments were promised for failure to comply. This does not mean there was no love motivation at all (as seen in such passages as Deuteronomy 6:5, Psalm 18:1, and Psalm 31:23).[3] But fear and conformity predominated in the people's relationship with God. Under grace, fear is banished by intimate fellowship with a loving God.

Over three decades ago J. F. Strombeck exposed the bankruptcy of fear as a motive in Christian living. He wrote:

A sinister influence, often offered as a motive for Christian conduct, is fear: fear of God's vengeance on the day of judgment, of being lost, of being forever cast out by God unless certain standards of life, often man made, are maintained. Fear is a desire to avoid or flee from that which causes harm. It is the natural feeling produced by the instinct of self-preservation. Self-preservation depends upon self to preserve; but he who sees, in grace, God's loving care for His own, and places his trust in Him, does not rely on self-preservation. Then fear is banished.[4]

The absence of fear is, of course, only one side of the coin. Once fear is removed, something must take its place. Scripture clearly teaches that this ingredient is love (2 Tim. 1:7; 1 John 4:17-18). Speaking of the motive of love in the economy of grace, Strombeck states: "Love must be the motive for all things done in response to grace."[5] The fear of God as a righteous judge is totally replaced by a motivation of love under the covenant of grace. God never uses the fear of punishment to motivate His children.[6]

This five-point contrast between law and grace should make clear the advantage of relating to God by grace. The law, with its statement of God's divine standards, its threats of judgment, and its conditional acceptance, could never make men holy. It was designed to reveal our guilt (Rom. 3:9-20) and to teach us our need of grace in Christ (Gal. 3:24-25). But it was not designed to mature us into righteousness.

The law was much like a sign that reads: "Wet Paint: Do Not Touch." It evoked our sinful propensities. In fact, Paul tells us the law actually caused us to sin more. "The law was added so that the trespass might increase. But where sin increased, grace increased all the more" (Rom. 5:20). The law was given to make our sins so obvious and our inability to merit divine acceptance so apparent that we would be driven to Christ's atonement and God's solution—a life of grace.

If we pause to think about it, we realize that only a relationship of grace can produce deep inner change in our personalities. The law can tell us God's standards. It may provoke rebellion. And it can even produce conformity, but the motivation for this comes from fear or guilt. God takes no pleasure in external conformity, as David wrote:

> You do not delight in sacrifice, or I would bring it;
>   you do not take pleasure in burnt offerings.
> The sacrifices of God are a broken spirit;
>   a broken and contrite heart,
>   O God, you will not despise.
>   (Ps. 51:16-17)

God wants a radical change in our inner attitude. He wants our love. And He knows that love is a response to being loved. John wrote:

> Let us love one another, for love comes from God. Everyone who loves has been born of God and knows God. Whoever does not love does not know God, because God is love. . . . There is no fear in love. But perfect love drives out fear, because fear has to do with punishment. The man who fears is not made perfect in love. We love because he first loved us. (1 John 4:7-8, 18-19)

Love is what God wants from us, for He knows that love will result in obedience and service. Conditional love, good works for blessings, and fear of punishment can produce conformity but not love. And love is the thing that law can never produce. Love comes only from the gratitude inspired by grace. Once we fully understand the extent of God's love for us and the unlimited measure of His grace, we cannot help but feel lasting gratitude. God's love pierces to the depth of our being and strikes a responsive chord of love. That is the ultimate impulse of all our positive responses to Him.

Law and Grace in Parenting

With this brief survey of the role of grace in Christian growth and discipline, we can turn now to its application in the parent-child relationship. We can follow one of two approaches in dealing with our children. We can follow principles of law or of grace. If we follow principles of law, we will focus on external conformity; we will demand a certain level of performance before we accept our children; we will withhold blessings until we are satisfied with our child's achievements; and we will rely on fear as a means to motivate them. In short, we will operate more as judges or police officers in our relations with our children.

When we observe families we see this is exactly the way most of us treat our children. Don't most of us, for example, focus more on external behavior than inner attitudes? We emphasize dress, hair, looks, friends, chores, grades, and other indicators of performance. If our children are performing well at school, if they dress appropriately, if they act mannerly, and if they complete their chores around the house, we assume that things are going well. But how many of us focus on our children's inner life—their feelings, thoughts, attitudes, and wishes? Yet this is the most important focus. Good deeds that are done with a negative attitude or out of negative motivation are of little value.

And don't most of us exhibit conditional love and conditional acceptance of our children? When they live the way we like, we are more open, loving, and affirming. When they fail to follow our directions or when they are grumpy and ill-mannered, our tempers flare and we feel less loving. In fact, we may even withhold a child's allowance or retaliate in other ways by withholding blessings in order to "bring them into line." All of these reactions are based on principles of law.

In contrast, those of us who follow God's example of grace will accept our children unconditionally. We will be concerned about our child's inner life. We will freely bestow blessings. And we will cultivate motivation by love. Such parents have learned the most important concept in rearing children. We do not produce righteousness and growth in children through punishment, pressure, and enforced conformity. Righteousness and growth in children are the natural fruit of our gracious and loving treatment. Our ultimate goal for our children is their love for God and others. This love is largely the product of our love for them. While parental punishment and hostility may produce external conformity, it is harmful to love and true holiness. Love, obedience, and commitment grow in response to unconditional love, unstinting patience, and unlimited forgiveness.

A hypothetical case will illustrate this point. Take two children and place one in a fear-oriented, externally focused, conditionally accepting family. This child learns to "be good" because she (or he) fears her parents' will reject her. She obeys to avoid punishment. If she steps out of line her mother or father will retaliate in anger, punish her severely, or imply she is "bad." Throughout her childhood and adolescent years this child is basically conforming. But inwardly she harbors deep resentment or she feels lonely and depressed. She has an active fantasy life and wishes she could be free of many inhibitions. But she doesn't rebel because of fear of punishment or rejection or because of guilt or shame.

As an adult this person either rejects restraints or continues to conform, all the while feeling empty and shallow. Years later she tells her parents, "Dad and Mom, I obeyed you for years. I conformed to your standards because I knew you would punish me severely if I stepped out of line or because I'd feel so guilty if I did. And I never sassed you because I knew that you wouldn't stand for it."

What satisfaction would parents gain from this? Would they

think their goal had been reached? While som
hear this as a compliment, I hope you hear a
child shows no depth of love and gratitude; the pau..
no understanding of maturity and trust.

Contrast this to a girl (or boy) reared in a loving, affirming home. Her parents set standards and they corrected, but out of love rather than anger and a fearful spirit. This child grows up and dialogues with her parents: "Dad and Mom, I love you. I want you to know I haven't always followed your directions, but I have learned. I am grateful that you were always for me. Even when I failed I knew that you cared. That helped me recognize my mistakes. Now I realize how helpful you were and I want to be the same way."

This child is a product of the parents' grace. She didn't always follow their counsel, but she knew they always supported her. Strengthened by this confidence she grew in love. Now she has learned the wisdom of their counsel and gladly serves them out of love and deep appreciation. The difference grace can make is inestimable. Grace produces inner health and outer beauty. It is a power for maturity and Christian character.

Summary

When a child misbehaves, we can react from one of two perspectives. If we operate from a legalistic view, we punish. We become angry because our standards were violated and law seems more vital than love. We will probably try to gain conformity to our wishes by generating fear and pressure.

In contrast, if we operate from grace we will see our children's failures as an opportunity to exhibit God's forgiveness and help. We will desire no revenge because our heart is filled with love. We accept our children unconditionally because we have been fully accepted by God. We will be concerned about developing their inner life because we are concerned about these things in our own life. And we will not resort to fear to motivate our children because we ourselves have been freed from fear by love.

-9-

A CHILD'S VIEW OF GOD

Of all parental opportunities and responsibilities, perhaps the most awesome is the responsibility to teach children about the character of God. The people of Israel were repeatedly exhorted to tell their children the wondrous things that God had done (Exod. 10:1-2; Deut. 4:9; Ps. 78:1-4; Isa. 38:19). By informing their children and grandchildren how God had delivered them from slavery in Egypt and had protected and provided for them in the wilderness, the Israelites were communicating to their children something of the character of God. And by teaching God's commandments and instructions (Deut. 6:1-2) they were telling a great deal more about His character.

But these narratives and instructions transmit only a partial knowledge of God. The child's understanding of God is both intellectual and experiential. In His wisdom, God ordained the family unit to impart to children a first-hand experience of His own fatherly character. Just as Scripture uses material illustrations like bread (John 6:30-35), light (John 1:1-9), and the vine (John 15:1-8) to illuminate aspects of divine truth, God designed the family as the instrument to communicate truths about His nature.

The Parental Image

The earliest concept of God in children emanates from their perception of their parents. Long before children have the ability to understand an unseen God, they are forming relationships with their parents, and these relationships result in deep patterns of understanding. These early patterns go a long way in shaping the young child's view of God.

Andrew Murray wrote concerning fathers:

> In the life he imparts to his child, in the image he sees reflected, in the unity of which he is conscious, in the loving care he exercises, in the obedience and the trust he sees given to himself, in the love in which family life finds happiness, the home and the fatherhood on earth are the image of the heavenly.[1]

Murray goes on to say that family life can point us to God:

> Every deeper insight into the Father's love and the Father's home would elevate the home on earth and enlarge our expectations of the blessing God, who appointed it, will certainly bestow upon it. Every experience of the love and blessing of a home on earth can be a ladder by which to rise up and get nearer the great Father-heart in heaven.[2]

Richard Strauss asks:

> What kind of God-concept is our child cultivating by his relationship with us? Is he learning that God is loving, kind, patient, and forgiving? Or are we unintentionally building a false image of God into his life, implying by our actions that God is harsh, short-tempered, and critical, that He nags us, yells at us, or knocks us around when we get out of line? Our children's entire spiritual life is at stake here. It is imperative that we learn what kind of parent God is, then follow His example in order that our children may see a living object lesson of the kind of God we have.[3]

A number of recent studies have demonstrated the connection between a person's image of God and one's concept of his or her parents. One of these studies showed that there was a greater similarity between the God and parent concepts in persons who were converted to Christianity before the age of ten than there was in people who experienced conversion after the age of seventeen.[4] Another study found that children relate the characteristics of both their mother and father to their concept of God.[5] This conclusion (confirmed in other studies) is consistent with Scripture's depiction of God as having both maternal and paternal characteristics.

> "O Jerusalem, Jerusalem, you who kill the prophets and stone those sent to you, how often I have longed to gather your children together, as a hen gathers her chicks under her wings, but you were not willing!" (Luke 13:34)

> A father to the fatherless, a defender of widows,
>   is God in his holy dwelling.
> God sets the lonely in families,
>   he leads forth the prisoners with singing;
>   but the rebellious live in a sun-scorched land.
>   (Ps. 68:5-6)

Mothers and fathers share the responsibility of demonstrating God's character to their children. By themselves, neither the typical masculine characteristics nor the typical feminine characteristics adequately reflect the diverse attributes of God. Some traits of God's character are best reflected by men, others by women.

Parental Hangovers

God's provision for teaching children about His character through relationships with parents means that we can strongly influence our child's concept of God in either a positive or a negative direction. Just as loving, sensitive parents make it easy for children to comprehend that God is sensitive and loving, critical and temperamental parents will predispose children to picture God as a negative, harsh person.

J. B. Phillips in his helpful book *Your God Is Too Small* wrote of several misconceptions of God that parents are likely to communicate to their children:

This early conception of God is almost invariably founded upon the child's idea of his father. If he is lucky enough to have a good father, that is all to the good, provided of course that the conception of God grows with the rest of personality. But if the child is afraid (or, worse still, afraid and feeling guilty because he *is* afraid of his own father) the chances are that his Father in heaven will appear to him a fearful Being. Again, if he is lucky, he will outgrow this conception and indeed differentiate between his early "fearful" idea and his later mature conception. But many are not able to outgrow the sense of guilt and fear, and in adult years are still obsessed with it, although it has actually nothing to do with their real relationship with the living God. It is nothing more than a parental hangover.[6]

Phillips goes on to describe other common misconceptions of God that are based on inadequate parent-child relations. He speaks of God as "resident policeman," "grand old man," "meek and mild," "heavenly bosom," and "managing director."

We could add others; for example, "cosmic killjoy," "great guilt machine," or "distant father." Each of these misconceptions has its roots in children's early relations with their parents. They are then either compounded or gradually corrected in the light of children's later experiences in the Christian culture and their own spiritual and emotional maturing. It seems likely, however, that these deeply ingrained misconceptions are never entirely expelled. Even those who have a firm intellectual understanding of the nature and attributes of God occasionally slip back into responding to God on the basis of these longstanding distortions.

Christian literature frequently reflects misconceptions of the character of God. Consider the concepts of God portrayed in the following paragraphs written to Christian parents.

Recently [God] made me ill for three weeks because I was not doing my homework. I was getting lazy and lax in my prayer life. Actually, He told me I was not being a good, strong, militant soldier in prayer, and I was not fighting in prayer as I should.

> When I was a little boy on the farm, one of our neighbors said he could tell his mule in a gentle voice to be obedient and the mule would be obedient. I wanted to see this, so I went over and asked him to show me how he controlled his mule so easily. He proceeded to get a big two-by-four and beat the mule. When he finished beating it, I asked him why he did that. He told me that was to get the mule's attention, and now he was going to talk to him. This is what God often does to me, only He gets my attention through illness.[7]

According to this view God is stern and punitive. He makes us ill for weeks when we neglect our prayer life. He sees us as stubborn mules. We might conclude from this that God delights in inflicting serious illness on His children to get their attention.

It is revealing that we read in the next paragraph:

> "When my dad spanked me once in front of my eighteen-year-old friends because I lied, I learned not only to repent for my sin, but that God and my father meant business."[8]

Here we see a person with a father who relied on severe physical discipline, and as a consequence this person believes that God punishes His children with physical pain. While physical pain may be a part of our growth as God's children, it does not happen in the crude and punitive manner this author suggests.

At the other end of the continuum, some authors present God as an overprotective mother to whom weak children flee in order to avoid the realities of life. This concept is found in many well-known hymns, including the following:

> Jesus, lover of my soul,
>   let me to Thy bosom fly,
> While the nearer waters roll,
>   while the tempest still is high!
> Hide me, O my Savior, hide—
>   till the storm of life is past;
> Safe into the haven guide,
>   O receive my soul at last![9]

Here we see Jesus pictured as a protective mother who shields helpless children from the stress of life. It is true, of course, that God protects His children, but His protection is quite different from this flight from strife. Phillips states:

Here, if the words are taken at their face value, is sheer escapism, a deliberate desire to be hidden safe away until the storm and stress of life is over, and no explaining away by lovers of the hymn can alter its plain sense. It can hardly be denied that if this is true Christianity, then the charge of "escapism," of emotional immaturity and childish regression must be frankly conceded. But although this "God of escape" is quite common, the true Christian course is set in a very different direction. No one would accuse its Founder of immaturity in insight, thought, teaching, or conduct, and the history of the Christian Church provides thousands of examples of timid half-developed personalities who have not only found in their faith what psychologists call integration, but have coped with difficulties and dangers in a way that makes any gibe of "escapism" plainly ridiculous.[10]

The Biblical Image

We are now ready to turn to the biblical view of the nature and the attributes of God. It is here, in a careful study of God's personality, that we find some of the richest truths for a comprehensive Christian view of parenting. Here we see both a model for our parenting and the importance of portraying God's character in our relationships with our children.

In modeling our character after God's, we must be careful to avoid either of two extremes. On the one hand, we may be tempted to deny or ignore God's attributes because we know we will fall short. "After all," we say, "we are only human." On the other hand, we can attempt to push the analogy beyond its limits. God's attributes are, in fact, infinite. They know no bounds or limitations, and they are perfect in every way. It *is* impossible therefore for us to fully comprehend His nature or to represent it perfectly. Sin in our life as well as innate human limitations make it impossible for us to fully represent God's character to our children. And certain of God's attributes have no close parallels in man.[11]

Between these two extremes we can steer a course that faithfully represents God's intent in establishing the responsibility of parents. We find that a large number of God's attributes are also given as goals for us to pursue, and we can be certain that we are not pushing the analogy beyond God's intent when we proceed in this way.

Although there are a variety of ways for categorizing biblical data on the character of God, I have chosen a tenfold presentation. This presentation is not intended to be exhaustive. In each instance we will first list a Scripture passage describing an aspect of God's character; this will be followed by a biblical injunction for demonstrating this attribute. Each section will conclude with comments on its relevance for parenting.

Holiness and Righteousness[12]

The holiness of God refers to His total separation from all that is sinful or evil. It affirms His complete perfection "in all that He is."[13] The righteousness of God refers to "that phase of the holiness of God which is seen in His treatment of the creature."[14] The Bible makes it clear that holiness and righteousness are fundamental attributes of God.

> "Holy, holy, holy is the Lord God Almighty, who was, and is, and is to come." (Rev. 4:8)

> The Lord is righteous in all His ways
> and loving toward all he has made.
> (Ps. 145:17)

Although no human being possesses the holiness that would commend us to God, we are nevertheless challenged to a life of holiness and righteousness:

> For God did not call us to be impure, but to live a holy life. (1 Thess. 4:7)

> LORD, who may dwell in your sanctuary?
> Who may live on your holy hill?
> He whose walk is blameless
> and who does what is righteous,
> who speaks the truth from his heart. . . .
> (Ps. 15:2)

The great gap between God's holiness and man's sinfulness makes it difficult to draw a close parallel between earthly fathers and the heavenly father. Yet purity and holiness are to be our standard and goal. A child's first glimpse of righteousness and holiness is seen in his parents. If these adults are committed to upright living, children will gain a positive picture of the righteousness of God and the desirability of a committed life.

Many children—especially teen-age boys—have tuned God out at least in part because of the counterfeit image of righteousness they saw in their parents or in the Christian subculture. Such righteousness (frequently called "spirituality") consists of withdrawal from the world, conformity to a list of external regulations, and passive conformity to convention. This spirituality, so far removed from positive, real living, neither attracts children to God nor strengthens its practitioners. While biblical righteousness includes the negative, it emphasizes the positive.

Another occasion for modeling the righteousness of God is the disciplining of our children (Prov. 22:15; Heb. 12:11). By lovingly correcting our children, we guide them in the path of righteousness.

Love[15]

Certainly love is one of the foremost attributes of God. His love is expressed to us in His grace, His mercy, and His longsuffering.

Whoever does not love does not know God, because God is love. (1 John 4:8)

O LORD, you preserve both man and beast.
    How priceless is your unfailing love!
Both high and low among men
    find refuge in the shadow of your wings.
(Ps. 36:6-7)

"In a surge of anger
    I hid my face from you for a moment,
but with everlasting kindness

I will have compassion on you,"
says the LORD your Redeemer.
                                    (Isa. 54:8)

And just as God is love, we are challenged to be filled with love.

"A new commandment I give you: Love one another. As
I have loved you, so you must love one another. All men
will know that you are my disciples if you love one
another." (John 13:34-35)

We should underscore a vital fact here concerning parents' love: parental attempts to live righteously and to model God's holiness apart from love are doomed to failure. Multitudes of young people have turned against their parents' Christianity because it affected much justice and little mercy. Paul states:

If I speak in the tongues of men and of angels, but have
not love, I am only a resounding gong or a clanging
cymbal. If I have the gift of prophecy and can fathom all
mysteries and all knowledge, and if I have a faith that can
move mountains, but have not love, I am nothing. If I
give all I possess to the poor and surrender my body to
the flames, but have not love, I gain nothing. (1 Cor.
13:1-3)

Nearly all parents love their children. But that is not sufficient. God so loved that He gave. Parents must take care to express their love in words and actions that children are able both to see and to understand. When mixed with righteousness and discipline, love is the powerful ingredient that serves as a bonding agent between the parent and child and ultimately between the child and God.

Fairness[16]

An aspect of God's righteousness that deserves special consideration is His fairness. The Bible speaks repeatedly of God being fair in all His dealings:

"Now let the fear of the LORD be upon you. Judge carefully, for with the LORD our God there is no injustice or
partiality or bribery." (2 Chron. 19:7)

Similarly, God's children are exhorted to fairness in all of their relations:

> But if you show favoritism, you sin and are convicted by the law as lawbreakers. (James 2:9)

In daily family interaction, we are repeatedly called upon to make judgments and decisions and to mediate between children. Many children learn to provoke a sibling in a sly manner and then clamor for justice on the "guilty party." We need to be wary of being drawn into the trap of favoring one child over another; this can disillusion a child on the matter of fairness.

To treat children fairly, of course, does not mean to treat them all alike. Children differ in many areas; their needs, make-ups, and capacities vary. They need impartial, considerate treatment that is suited to their particular situation.

Sensitivity and Gentleness [17]

God's love includes sensitivity and gentleness, and these aspects deserve our attention.

> For we do not have a high priest who is unable to sympathize with our weaknesses, but we have one who has been tempted in every way, just as we are—yet was without sin. (Heb. 4:15)

God is sensitive to our needs, and we are told to show the same awareness to others, including our children.

> Be kind and compassionate to one another, forgiving each other, just as in Christ God forgave you. (Eph. 4:32)

> Finally, all of you, live in harmony with one another, be sympathetic, love as brothers, be compassionate and humble. (1 Peter 3:8)

According to the Scriptures, God is always sympathetic to His people's needs. He "sympathizes" with us in our weaknesses. What a compelling example this is for us to sympathize with the confusions, struggles, and aspirations of our child! This human identification is possible because of the astonishing condescension of the Lord from heaven, which is

summarized in one commentary as follows: "In sympathy He
adapts Himself to each as if He had not merely taken on Him
man's nature in general, but also the peculiar nature of that
single individual."[18]

Humility[19]

> For by the grace given me I say to every one of you: Do
> not think of yourself more highly than you ought, but
> rather think of yourself with sober judgment, in accord-
> ance with the measure of faith God has given to you.
> (Rom 12:3)

We are given a lofty position in relation to our children. We
are given the authority to instruct (Deut. 6:1-9), train (Prov.
22:6), and correct (Prov. 13:24). And children are instructed
to be obedient (Eph. 6:1). Yet we have a model for humility in
the example of Christ. In spite of Christ's exalted position of
authority, He humbled Himself, was obedient to His father,
and served others. Similarly, parents, while occupying a position of authority over their children, should humble themselves by obedience and service—obedience to their Father,
and service to their children.

We should seek to be worthy of our children's love, respect, and admiration through our loving and humble service
rather than attempting to gain their respect through power.
Parental abuse of authority leads children to see all authority
(including God) as selfish or manipulative. A servant attitude
on our part gives our children a beautiful illustration of the
humble character of Christ and inspires youth toward service
to humanity.

Patience and Longsuffering[20]

> But for that very reason I was shown mercy so that in
> me, the worst of sinners, Christ Jesus might display his
> unlimited patience as an example for those who would
> believe on him and receive eternal life. (1 Tim. 1:16)

> The LORD is compassionate and gracious,
>   slow to anger, abounding in love.
>   (Ps. 103:8)

God's love encompasses His patience and longsuffering, and certainly these are parental virtues as well.

> And we urge you, brothers, warn those who are idle, encourage the timid, help the weak, be patient with everyone. (1 Thess. 5:14)

> My dear brothers, take note of this: Everyone should be quick to listen, slow to speak and slow to become angry, for man's anger does not bring about the righteous life that God desires. (James 1:19-20)

In an age of impulse and immediacy, we need to be reminded of the divine virtue of patience. What better way is there for a child to learn of God's loving forbearance than in the kindly patience of parents? Impulsive, capricious parents and those given to hostile outbursts instill a distorted image of God in the minds of their children. These children find it difficult to accept God's patient strength and are frequently afraid that God will unpredictably lose His temper and punish them for no known reason.

Encouragement[21]

Many Christians cannot picture God as freely encouraging His children. They may accept His holiness, His righteousness, His fairness, and perhaps even His love and patience—without comprehending that quality of generous support extended to His people in need. But Scripture asserts the reality of this support.

> May the God who gives endurance and encouragement give you a spirit of unity among yourselves as you follow Christ Jesus. (Rom. 15:5)

And we, too, are to practice this:

> Encourage one another daily, as long as it is called Today, so that none of you may be hardened by sins's deceitfulness. (Heb. 3:13)

The troubled child needs encouragement above all else. It is so easy to notice faults and to criticize, but it is so difficult to build up tottering personalities. With God as our example, we

can sense our children's struggles and fashion ways of
bolstering their sagging egos and encouraging them.

Forgiveness [22]

The forgiveness of God is graphically described in the Book
of Psalms:

> As far as the east is from the west,
>   so far has he removed our transgressions from us.
>   (Ps. 103:12)

And Jesus tells us what this means for our lives:

> Then Peter came to Jesus and asked, "Lord, how many
> times shall I forgive my brother when he sins against
> me? Up to seven times?" Jesus answered, "I tell you, not
> seven times, but seventy-seven times." (Matt. 18:21-22)

Guilt is a perennial problem for many Christians. In spite of
"knowing better," these Christians suffer the persistent an-
guish of continuing guilt. Their inability to experience God's
forgiveness can nearly always be traced to parents who did not
forgive and forget their children's failures. The resulting ap-
prehension and self-depreciation shrouds adult years and
makes it very difficult to believe in God's forgiveness.

Faithful and Trustworthy [23]

According to Scripture, God is always faithful:

> God, who has called you into fellowship with his Son
> Jesus Christ our Lord, is faithful (1 Cor. 1:9)

What God promises, He will do; and He prizes this integ-
rity in His people.

> A faithful man will be richly blessed,
>   but one eager to get rich will not go unpunished.
>   (Prov. 28:20)

A story is told of a father who placed his son on a table and
instructed him to "jump to daddy." The young lad did and the
father stepped away and let him fall. "That," the father said,
"will teach you not to trust anybody."

Other parents unwittingly teach their children not to trust people. They promise them an outing and at the last minute they cancel out. They love their children, but they do not take the time to listen to them. Such faithlessness plants doubt about the parents' reliability.

In later life this skepticism can carry over to the person's relationship with God; and it can be difficult for this person to believe His promises, especially when they aren't immediately fulfilled.

Changelessness

One of the great comforts in the Christian life is that we have an unchanging Father. God is not fickle; He is totally consistent with His perfect character at all times.

> In the beginning, O Lord, you laid the foundations of the earth, and the heavens are the work of your hands. They will perish, but you remain; they will all wear out like a garment. You will roll them up like a robe; like a garment they will be changed. But you remain the same, and your years will never end. (Heb. 1:10-12)

Nothing is more confusing to a child than inconsistent parents. Although we will never achieve perfection in this, parents need to strive for more predictability. Our children need to know what to expect from us. If their misbehavior is sometimes labled "cute" and smiled upon but later draws rebuke, they become confused. If we are sometimes approachable and sometimes unresponsive, this builds anxiety and fear. Parental vacillation and double-mindedness must be overcome if children are to become mature.

Summary

This concludes our survey of the major attributes of God that relate to Christian parenting. Needless to say, no parent will achieve perfection in any of these, but parental development toward these ideals will be reflected in the children. Paul holds our high Example before us:

> Be imitators of God, therefore, as dearly loved children
> and live a life of love, just as Christ loved us and gave
> himself up for us as a fragrant offering and sacrifice to
> God. (Eph. 5:1-2)

Just as we want our children to grow, we are to continue
maturing in the image of God—inwardly in the depths of our
personal lives. We should be quick to admit our failures and
faults to our children, but always progressing in the ways we
want our children to develop. As we do, we will reap the rich
reward of seeing our children draw near the loving, mighty
God in a personal-experiential way.

-10-

SELF-ESTEEM
IN
CHILDREN

Just as God uses parents to communicate His attributes to children, He also charges them to communicate knowledge of their children's true identity. It is in the home that children's first self-perceptions and evaluations take place, and it is here that children first learn to value and respect themselves or to belittle and reject themselves.

In our psychologically sophisticated society, most writers on child development stress the importance of a good self-concept. Dorothy Briggs calls self-esteem "the crucial ingredient" in a child's life. She writes, "If your child has self-esteem, he has it made."[1] James Dobson says, "The health of an entire society depends on the ease with which its individual members gain personal acceptance."[2] And William Homan says, "You could almost use a person's self-confidence as a measure of the success or failure of his whole life."[3]

Undoubtedly the attitudes children hold toward themselves are significant features of their total life adjustment. Yet the current emphasis on self-esteem, self-love, and self-acceptance raises some serious questions for both the student of Scripture and the Christian parent. Does the Bible, in fact, teach that we should love ourselves? Are there hazards in the current "self-acceptance" movement? Is there a biblical basis for a positive self-concept? And if there is, how do we reconcile biblical teachings on humility and pride with concepts of self-love and self-esteem? In the past few years many Christian authors have begun to say that we should develop positive attitudes about ourselves. Walter Trobisch, for example, writes:

> We find that the Bible confirms what modern psychology has recently discovered: without self-love there can be no love for others. Jesus equates these two loves, and binds them together, making them inseparable.[4]

And Robert Schuller states:

> I strongly suggest that self-love is the ultimate will of man—that what you really want more than anything else in the world is the awareness that you are a worthy person.[5]

Frequently, however, such statements on the Christian's self-esteem do not flow from a comprehensive view of Scripture. In fact, many have tried to erect a view of self-esteem almost solely on Christ's statement, "Love your neighbor as yourself" (Mark 12:31). They state that since Christ commands us to love our neighbors *as ourselves*, we must first, obviously, love ourselves.[6] Yet the primary intent of Christ's reply to the scribes is obviously not to exhort us to self-love. Christ had been asked, "Of all the commandments, which is the most important?"

> "The most important one," answered Jesus, "is this: 'Hear, O Israel, the Lord our God, the Lord is one. Love the Lord your God with all your heart and with all your soul and with all your mind and with all your strength.' The second is this: 'Love your neighbor as yourself.' " (Mark 12:29-31)

The clear message of this passage is that we are to love God and our neighbors. While the first sentence in verse 31 may indirectly lend support to a concept of self-love, it surely does not provide an adequate biblical foundation on which to erect a theology of self-esteem or self-acceptance.

If we turn from this passage, however, to the broad scope of Scripture, we do find a strong basis for a positive yet balanced self-esteem. This self-esteem is established on a threefold reality: God views all members of the human race as (1) highly significant, (2) deeply fallen, and (3) greatly loved.[7] To communicate that God values human life, parents need to teach and act in such a way that their children will recognize both their significance and their sinfulness, and all the while realize that they are loved by their Creator.

The Significance of Children

From the first chapter of Genesis to the last chapter of Revelation, the Bible stresses the high value God places on the human being. This worth is seen in Adam and Eve being created in God's image (Gen. 1:26-27). It is found in the Psalms where we are said to be "crowned . . . with glory and honor" (Ps. 8:5). And in the last chapter of Revelation we are told that redeemed persons will spend eternity with God. These and other biblical passages reveal at least six foundations for self-esteem.

"In His Image"

While attending a meeting of scholars, the famous literary critic Thomas Carlyle was asked to express his view on man's origin and descent. "Gentlemen," he declared, "you place man a little higher than the tadpole. I hold with the ancient singer, 'Thou hast made him a little lower than the angels!' "

Carlyle captured the ultimate source of self-esteem. Man is not merely an advanced animal, another link in the evolutionary chain; he is the sublime creation of the personal God. The fact that man was created in the image of God is the basis for a biblical doctrine of self-esteem. Schaeffer put it well:

> For twentieth-century man this phrase, the image of God, is as important as anything in Scripture, because man today can no longer answer that crucial question, "Who am I?" In his own naturalistic theories, with the uniformity of cause and effect in a closed system, with an evolutionary concept of a mechanical chance parade from

the atom to man, man has lost his unique identity. As he looks out upon the world, as he faces the machine, he cannot tell himself from what he faces. He cannot distinguish himself from the other things.[8]

It is a paradox that it is usually non-Christian philosophers and psychologists who emphasize man's need for self-esteem while Christian preachers and writers have frequently undermined this concept through a one-sided emphasis on humility, self-denial, and sin. If the secular theorist were consistent with his evolutionary view of human life, he would be led logically to despair and the ultimate meaninglessness of man. In contrast, if the Christian is consistent with the biblical concept of human creation in God's image, this leads to deep respect for humanity's significance and value. It is on this foundation that we must chart the pattern for a child's self-concept. The first thing God chose to reveal about us was that we are in His image!

A High Calling

God placed Adam and Eve in the Garden of Eden and told them to "be fruitful and increase in number; fill the earth and subdue it." Then He instructed them to "rule over the fish of the sea and the birds of the air and over every living creature that moves on the ground" (Gen. 1:29-31). Here we have a second sign of the significance of mankind: God commissioned Adam and Eve to have dominion over the earth. In referring to this passage, Erich Sauer writes:

> God had given man a high task. He was to administer the earth in the holy service of the Most High. He was to be the Creator's viceroy in this region of His created kingdom.[9]

God did not consider Adam a puppet or a weakling. He told him to name the various animals and to rule over the earth. In this vocation Adam and his descendants were to bring all of the earth under fruitful control. This divine assignment continues to expand today.

The Crown of Creation

Genesis records the sequence of God's creative acts. And it puts man at the peak. God started with the heavens and the earth, then introduced light, separated water and land and put plants in the soil, aligned the sun and moon with the earth for daily timekeeping, filled the seas with fish and the sky with fowl—and He observed that it all was good. But despite all this grandeur of design and production, there was still no creature to commune with the Creator. So God then made a man and a woman who could talk and work with Him.

Fellow personalities with God, we are the apex of His creation. We can communicate with Him, return His love, and share in His cosmic endeavors! That realization elicited the psalmist's intense praise: "What is man that you are mindful of him, the son of man that you care for him? You made him a little lower than the heavenly beings and crowned him with glory and honor" (Ps. 8:4-5).

Bought With a Price

Another overwhelming evidence of the significance of man is demonstrated in God's redemption of humanity.

> For you know that it was not with perishable things such as silver or gold that you were redeemed from the empty way of life handed down to you from your forefathers, but with the precious blood of Christ, a lamb without blemish or defect. (1 Peter 1:18-19)

The purchase price of an object attests to its value. After Adam's sin, Satan, not God, was the master of humanity; and death, not life, was humanity's destiny. Humanity was spiritually enslaved by the power of sin, and it lacked the spiritual riches to purchase freedom. Then Christ, the holy Son of God, intervened and offered His own perfect life on the cross in payment for the sinner's debt (Mark 10:45).

It is important to realize that while the value of human beings is *proved by* the inestimable sacrifice of Christ for their redemption, this value does not *come from* this redemption. Some Christians say, "Christians are valuable and should like themselves because they are identified with Christ." This is theologically inaccurate. Although the great truths of justification and union with Christ certainly influence the Christian's identity, they are not its original source. Our identity is rooted in our creation. God judged humanity so valuable that He gave His best to redeem man. Justification from sin and union with Christ speak of fellowship and forgiveness, but creation speaks to our basic significance, worth, and value.

Heavenly Guardians

A fifth reason for a positive self-evaluation is the fact that God appoints angels to minister to His people.

> For he will command his angels concerning you
> 　to guard you in all your ways;
> they will lift you up in their hands
> 　so that you will not strike your foot against a stone.
> 　　　　　　　　　　　　　　　　　　　(Ps. 91:11-12)

Although the two-hundred-plus Scripture references to angels do not explain their mission in detail, it is clear that they serve God's people at God's command. We are told, for example, that God sent an angel to shut the mouths of hungry lions when Daniel was thrown into their den (Dan. 6:22). Angels attended Jesus after He overcame Satan's temptations (Matt. 4:11). Christ said that little children have angels watching over them (Matt. 18:10). And the author of Hebrews reveals that angels are ministering spirits sent to render service to those who will inherit salvation (Heb. 1:14).

Ultimate Destination

Shortly before His crucifixion, Jesus consoled His disciples:

> "Do not let your hearts be troubled. Trust in God; trust also in me. In my Father's house are many rooms; if it were not so, I would have told you. I am going there to prepare a place for you. And if I go and prepare a place for you, I will come back and take you to be with me that you also may be where I am." (John 14:1-3)

The promise of eternity with God is a final and crowning evidence of the believer's worth to God. God sees humanity to be of such value and significance that He planned an eternity in our company. These biblical bases for self-esteem apply to every member of the human race. They provide a solid foundation for a positive identity. A special value, however, attaches to children in Scripture. When the disciples attempted to turn away little children so that Jesus would have more time for adults, He rebuked them: "Let the little children come to me, and do not hinder them, for the kingdom of heaven belongs to such as these" (Matt. 19:14).

B. B. Warfield summarizes Christ's attitude toward children in this way:

> He illustrated the ideal of childhood in His own life as a child. He manifested the tenderness of His affection for children by conferring blessings upon them in every stage of their development as He was occasionally brought in contact with them. He asserted for children a recognized place in His kingdom, and dealt faithfully and lovingly with each age as it presented itself to him in the course of His work. He chose the condition of childhood as a type of the fundamental character of the recipients of the kingdom of God. He adopted the relation of childhood as the most vivid earthly image of the relation of God's people to Him who was not ashamed to be called their Father which is in heaven, and thus reflected back upon this relation a glory by which it has been transfigured ever since.[10]

If we are to follow Jesus' example, we must ascribe high significance and value to all children.

Sin and Self-esteem

The significance of man to God as the foundation for a positive self-image is, of course, only one side of the coin. Scripture speaks just as clearly to the presence of sin and the fact that God-imaged man is not living up to his created potential.

As it is written:
"There is no one righteous, not even one."
(Rom. 3:10)
Who may ascend the hill of the LORD?
Who may stand in His holy place?
He who has clean hands and a pure heart. . . .
(Ps. 24:3-4)

The fact that everyone has sinned against God is also relevant to proper self-esteem. The Bible instructs us not to think more highly of ourselves than we ought (Rom. 12:3), and we are warned that "pride goes before destruction, a haughty spirit before a fall" (Prov. 16:18). These and other passages expose our guilt in overestimating ourselves—in considering ourselves more important than other people or God. This pride results in a false self-worth that militates against recognition of our true worth in God.

Some teachers and writers imply that sin wipes out all of the significance and value we possessed at Creation. This is not the case. The fall into sin destroyed our righteousness and made it impossible for any of us to meet the standards of divine holiness. But a lack of righteousness is very different from a lack of worth. Sin blights, estranges, and eventually kills, but God's implanted image gives sustained significance to the sinner with saint-potential.[11]

Christian parents helping their children to see themselves as God sees them will not shirk the responsibility of teaching right from wrong and correcting them when they fall short. At the same time we must be careful to view our children's *sinfulness* within the bounds of their *significance*. Many parents, in emphasizing their children's sins and failures, give the impression that their basic characteristic is that of being evil.

Constant focus on children's misdeeds causes them to repress their natural sense of worth, leading them to erect their self-evaluation on the wrong foundation. Seeing themselves primarily as failures or sinners rather than God's image-bearers, they have great difficulty accepting their positive attributes and possibilities. Lacking confidence, they find any expression of their significance at odds with their assumed identity. Down on themselves, they overtly or covertly put others down, and this negativism spreads like a cancer. We need to communicate an awareness of our child's sinfulness, but this must *follow* an understanding of the child's significance and value. The first and most basic thing about human nature is that it is created in God's image. Although seriously distorted, this image of God is not destroyed. The fact that Christ gave His life for us while we were mired in sin shows our value and significance. Sin is deadly, but it is foreign to our original nature and only a temporary scourge. It did not exist in human nature before the Fall, and it will be banished at the end of this life for those who love God. In the meantime, no matter how spiritually tainted and crippled they are, God's creatures are still significant to Him; and we should communicate this to our children.

Helping children develop self-esteem should not be looked at as an isolated goal or an end in itself, as in humanistic approaches. For the Christian, self-esteem is only one part of a total biblical world view that includes the right attitude toward oneself, God, and others. This requires care in avoiding accusatory speech, condemning attitudes, and actions that indicate disrespect for others. Self-respect coexists with a wholesome regard for all humanity.

Ingredients of Self-esteem

The Bible lays a foundation for a positive and balanced self-concept, but it does not spell out in detail the psychological elements. Psychologists, however, generally agree that all children need a sense of security, of worth, of confidence, and of belonging or being loved. Since God as our heavenly Father provides each of these for His children, these four ingredients of a positive self-concept should be the goal of every parent. These were treated in the discussion of children's needs in chapter 5, so we will not develop them further here except to note that the typical parent has a number of attitudes, habits, and patterns of communication that tend to undermine children's self-esteem. As parents we all need to make a continuing, concerted effort to instill a sense of security, confidence, worth, and love in our children.

Pride, Humility, and Self-esteem

Some of us hesitate to promote our children's self-esteem for fear of fostering sinful pride. To avoid this problem, we need a clear understanding of the biblical definition of pride. Sinful pride involves a threefold attitude. *Toward themselves* proud persons feel self-sufficient. They trust in their own accomplishments and assets while denying their need of others. *Toward God* they exhibit arrogance. Based on an overestimation of their abilities, they deny their need of God. To them God is but a crutch for weak people. *Toward others* they are scornful or indifferent. They minimize others.

The New Testament concept of pride literally means "haughty" or "lifted up." It suggests an inflated opinion of oneself—much like a balloon filled with air. This pride is far from the approval or satisfaction a person feels as a result of a positive identity. Humility does not rule out self-regard and self-respect; it simply asks that we value others the same way we esteem ourselves. This is why Christ said, "Love your neighbor as yourself" (Mark 12:31).

Just as the sin of pride is totally different from self-acceptance, humility is completely different from a low self-estimation. Humility is neither inferiority, underestimation of our abilities, nor self-hatred. Paul gives us a model:

> Your attitude should be the same as that of Christ Jesus:
> Who, being in very nature God,
> did not consider equality with God something
> to be grasped,
> but made himself nothing,
> taking the very nature of a servant,
> being made in human likeness.
> And being found in appearance as a man,
> he humbled himself
> and became obedient to death—
> even death on a cross!
> Therefore God exalted him to the highest place. . . .
> (Phil. 2:5-9)

Earlier in Philippians 2 Paul urges the church to be unified and warns the Philippians about the dangers of sinful pride. He speaks first of (1) being like-minded, (2) having the same love, and (3) being one in spirit and purpose. Then he mentions the attitudes that can ruin this unity—selfishness and conceit. Paul writes, "In humility consider others better than yourselves" (v. 2).

Then, in the passage quoted above, Paul goes on to explain what this humility consists of. This passage gives four aspects of Christ's humility:

1. He had a high position.
2. He took a position low in service but high in worth.
3. He was obedient even to death.
4. He was exalted after His death.

This, says Paul, is our example of humility. Notice the absence of any feelings of inferiority or self-degrading statements. Christ certainly did not see Himself as inferior or worthless in the sight of other men. He knew His value, His worth, and His identity. Since He had a secure identity, He didn't have to flaunt His strengths; He was free to put aside His prerogatives for the benefit of others. The essence of humility hinges on that point. Even though Christ was God, He willingly humbled Himself, became a servant, and obeyed His Father in all aspects of His earthly life. Our humility should be the same. In fact, there are some striking parallels. Notice that we, like Christ:

1. have a high position as God's children and image-bearers;
2. can take a position low in service but high in worth;
3. can be obedient to God until our death;
4. will be exalted after our death as we reign with Christ forever.

When Paul told us to esteem ourselves below others, He was not impugning our worth or assigning us to inferiority. Instead, he was saying that as people with a secure identity, we can focus on the needs of others; we can be ministering to them.

Biblical humility connotes our realistic evaluation of ourselves and our ability (Rom. 12:3), acknowledgment of our need of God (Deut. 8), and a readiness to serve (Luke 22:25-26). In no instance is biblical humility equated with self-rejection or an inadequate self-concept.

In teaching children to respect others—without downgrading themselves—to carry out their own share of responsibility, to help others willingly, and to recognize their personal need of God, we train them in aspects of humility. And as we generously serve our children's needs we are modeling the humility Paul challenged the church to exercise. This humility is a trait of the spiritually mature and a psychologically healthy expression issuing from a positive identity.

Building Self-esteem

Since our primary purpose in this book is to trace the biblical patterns of child rearing, we will not provide in-depth methods of building a child's self-esteem. We can, however, list some brief guidelines for concerned parents:

1. Spend mutually enjoyable time together.
2. Compliment freely and sincerely.
3. Value a child's ideas and emotions.
4. Correct in love.
5. Communicate respect.
6. Curtail criticism.
7. Avoid guilt motivation.
8. Don't demean a child's character.
9. Encourage and support.
10. Avoid overprotection.
11. Communicate God's high valuation of the child.

These guides for daily practice will build deep feelings of personal respect and worth in children and move them along to the biblical view of themselves, of God, and of others.

-11-

COMMUNICATION BRIDGES AND BARRIERS

Good communication is fundamental in every area of child rearing. Without communication we fail to convey love to children. Without communication we instruct and discipline ineptly. And without communication children miss the biblical concepts of their noble identity and their potential relationship with God.

Most of us take the process of communication for granted until short circuits set off explosions. Less than ideal patterns of communication may yield tolerable results, despite occasional sparks, but the latent failure becomes evident when tempers erupt in angry revolt or spirits shrivel in silent rejection.

In dealing with this relational network, we will draw heavily on the wisdom literature of Proverbs. We will begin with four positive elements of effective communication—four attitudes that build bridges to our children, then we will consider three attitudes and actions that undermine meaningful communication. In sketching this biblical pattern we are not presenting a treatise on communication skills such as is found in specialized volumes on the subject.[1] Our purpose here is to gain a broad perspective.

Listening

The starting point for effective communication is listening. Perhaps more than any other factor, listening is the key to opening channels of understanding with our children. Unless our children know that they are heard, they keep their innermost selves hidden. They talk *at* us or *to* us instead of *with* us. The universal tendency of human beings is to speak—not to listen. We all want to tell others—especially our children—what we think. Priding ourselves on our knowledge, experience, or authority we believe we can help our children most by telling or instructing. Telling certainly has its place, yet listening is the key. Through listening we win a hearing. Proverbs says:

> He who answers before listening—
> that is his folly and his shame.
> (Prov. 18:13)

And James writes:

> My dear brothers, take note of this: Everyone should be quick to listen, slow to speak, and slow to become angry. (James 1:19)

When our children come home from school upset, when they "forget" to do their chores, when they fuss and fight, and when they seem completely uncooperative, our natural impulse is to challenge or chastise them. But almost without fail our words do little to resolve the real problem. In times of tension as well as in times of calm, children yearn for a sympathetic ear. Parents who can quench their impulse to "set their child straight" long enough to draw out the child by listening will be richly rewarded.

Empathy

Closely akin to listening is the ability to see things from our children's perspective. An Indian prayer asks, "Help me not to criticize my brother until I have walked a mile in his moccasins." From the hurt finger of a three-year-old to the desolation of a teen-ager whose love affair has ended, parents should try to put themselves in their children's shoes. We need to remember how difficult a child's world can be in order to learn to share their struggles.

We may think of childhood as a time of play, but new experiences and soaring expectations that may or may not be fulfilled are much more than mere play. Children must cope with rejection by their peers. They must face critical or insensitive teachers. And they must learn to handle hours of boredom, anxiety over sexuality, and a host of other challenges. Parents who want deep communication take these situations seriously. They try to place themselves in their children's setting, see things from their perspective, and empathize with their concerns. Like Jesus, they are able to "sympathize with our [child's] weaknesses" (Heb. 4:15).

The ability to feel with our children and understand their inner lives has been beautifully modeled for us by God. The Scripture tells us that the Holy Spirit helps us in our weaknesses by interceding for us "with groans that words cannot express" (Rom. 8:26). God even knows our needs before we ask (Matt. 6:8). And Christ's willingness to give up His position in heaven to walk with man demonstrates His total identification with our struggles. Christ did not sit idly by and lecture, threaten, or condemn us. He took on our likeness (Rom. 8:3), suffered our temptations (Heb. 4:15), and personally experienced our sorrows (Isa. 53:3-5).

Christ can deeply identify with our struggles because He was there. Similarly, Christian parents are called to identify with the sufferings and struggles of their children. They need to step into their children's world and absorb the hurts, confusion, and grief. They also need to experience their joys and excitement. When this deep understanding is developed, it is unlikely that serious problems will suddenly jeopardize the relationship.

Timely Talk

A man finds joy in giving an apt reply—
and how good is a timely word!
(Prov. 15:23)

The heart of the righteous weighs its answers,
but the mouth of the wicked gushes evil.
(Prov. 15:28)

Do you see a man who speaks in haste?
There is more hope for a fool than for him.
(Prov. 29:20)

Listening is only one half of the communication circuit. Children also need fitting words of encouragement, instruction, and support. And the timing of these words is important. How frequently we regret an ill-timed word. Words spoken impulsively or in anger can wound. They tear down our children's self-esteem and cut away at positive attitudes. And even right words wrongly timed can rob our children of important self-discoveries or rob us of the opportunity to share their deep concerns. Well-chosen and well-timed words are wisdom in action.

Openness and Honesty

Therefore confess your sins to each other and pray for each other so that you may be healed. (James 5:16)

Do not lie to each other, since you have taken off your old self with its practices. (Col. 3:9)

Scripture places a premium on honesty. Yet we sometimes fail to see how important an open attitude and an honest spirit are to effective communication. Without honesty we have no basis for mutual respect and trust. By honesty we mean not only the refusal to lie but also the commitment not to hide the truth. And we mean an attitude of openness that freely acknowledges our own failures and reveals our true feelings.

Nagging

One of the easiest ruts for us to slip into is to nag. When our children fail to carry through on a household task or a school assignment, we begin to "remind" them. Then our promptings escalate to fretful nagging. Gradually we add accusing terms, saying things like, "What's the matter with you?" "I've

told you a hundred times!" Or "I can't count on you for anything!" We badger them about messy rooms. We fuss about
dress and eating habits. And we pester them about chores not
done. This is one of the quickest ways to shut off communication. Children quickly learn to "tune out" the grating tone
that carries the note of defeat. They may even get some pleasure out of seeing how upset we get over their "forgetfulness"!
The Bible speaks clearly to the effectiveness of nagging—it
doesn't work! While we need to motivate our children to
improve their behavior, nagging is not the way. Repetitious,
shrill instruction is a sign of bad communication, poor training, parental inconsistency, or some form of futile discipline.
It is a sign to stop, ponder the breakdown, and start over.

Quarreling

It is to a man's honor to avoid strife,
but every fool is quick to quarrel.
(Prov. 20:3)

Quarreling is another habit that destroys communication. A
big brother of nagging, quarreling is a somewhat more obvious and open form of inadequate communication. While not
as blatant as an outright fight or a fit of rage, quarreling cor-
rodes respect and trust. It clogs channels of communication
and may warn of a coming rupture. The wise and loving parent refuses to allow a disagreement to expand into a quarrel.

Anger

The problems of nagging and quarreling lead us directly to
the matter of anger. Anger is perhaps the biggest barrier to
effective communication. It blurs reason, generates fear, and
stirs up further strife. Communication is difficult if not impossible when there is anger in our action and speech. Because of the ravages of anger, we will delve into its nature and
effects and examine some of the ways to resolve it.

Many writers today defend anger. They say it is "unavoid-
able," "constructive," "neutral," and a "normal" human emotion. One author, for example, writes: "The Bible does not

condemn anger. On the contrary we read, 'Be angry and sin not'" (Eph. 4:26, KJV).[2]

Granted, anger is a universal human experience and we cannot deny its presence, even in mature Christians. Some believers *have* been pushed into depression and self-hatred by parents and religious leaders who naïvely taught that real Christians do not experience anger. This repression, we have learned, is the source of many personal adjustment problems. It is a root of depression. It underlies much anxiety. And it is a causal factor in some psychosomatic problems such as headaches, ulcers, and low back pains.

But a careful study of Scripture does not support the belief that most anger is not sin. In fact, there is only one passage (Eph. 4:26) that directly suggests that anger is not sin. In contrast, we read in Colossians 3:8: "But now you must rid yourselves of all such things as these: anger, rage, malice, slander, and filthy language from your lips." There are numerous such passages that condemn anger and instruct us to put it away (Prov. 14:29; 15:1; 15:18; 25:15; Rom. 12:19; 2 Cor. 12:20; Eph. 4:31; 1 Tim. 2:8; James 1:19-20). According to these verses, most anger compounds trouble and fails to produce the righteousness of God. It is to be resolved along with other sins such as slander, gossip, arrogance, and malice.

Then how can we reconcile Ephesians 4:26 and countless biblical references to God's anger with all of these passages that encourage us to put away anger? The answer is that there is a righteous anger and a sinful anger. Christ was angry in the temple confrontation with "robbers" (Matt. 21:12-13), and Scripture clearly shows God's anger against the wicked. But there is a vast difference between God's righteous anger and most human anger. The first characteristic of righteous anger is that it is always directed toward evil (and agents of evil).

> See, the day of the LORD is coming
> —a cruel day, with wrath and fierce anger—
> to make the land desolate
> and destroy the sinners within it.
> (Isa. 13:9)

God's righteous anger is a just response to evil, but most human anger is directed toward people or actions that frustrate our desires, interfere with our expectations, or disturb our comfort. Consider a person driving on the freeway, for example. He is in a hurry and is driving in the left lane. The driver just ahead is obeying the speed limit, but our knight of the road is late for an appointment and he "needs" to exceed the 55-mile-per-hour speed limit. He becomes irritated because the driver ahead won't move over and let him by. Resentment, recriminations, perhaps even rage and reckless maneuvers issue from him. Chances are he believes he's justified in his resentment. He thinks, *Doesn't he know the left lane is for those who want to break the limit?* Here is a classic example of believing one's anger is "righteous" and "justified." But he is angry at someone who is obeying the law, and the real cause of his anger is that it frustrates his own desires. This isn't righteous indignation!

A second distinction between righteous and sinful anger is: righteous anger coexists with love and a concern for the other person's welfare. God loves us and wants the best for us, even while we are in sin.

> The Lord is not slow in keeping his promise, as some understand slowness. He is patient with you, not wanting anyone to perish, but everyone to come to repentance. (2 Peter 3:9)

Just as God loves the sinner even though He becomes righteously indignant about sin, righteous human anger will coexist with constructive love and a concern for the other's best. Unfortunately, most times when we are angry we do not lovingly desire the other person's best. In fact, most of the times that we are angry we secretly (or sometimes not so secretly) hope that something bad or painful will happen to the person we resent.

A third difference between righteous and unrighteous anger is that righteous anger does not involve revenge.

> Do not repay anyone evil for evil. Be careful to do what is right in the eyes of everybody. If it is possible, as far as

it depends on you, live at peace with everyone. Do not take revenge, my friends, but leave room for God's wrath, for it is written: "It is mine to avenge, I will repay," says the Lord. (Rom. 12:17-19)

According to Scripture, God has reserved to Himself the right to pass out punishment. At its core, anger is a desire to gain revenge or get even with someone we believe has offended us. The essence of sinful anger is our desire to usurp God's role and take justice into our own hands. Rather than accepting the fact that God has graciously forgiven the people we resent and knowing that their sin will be handled in the future, we want to see them receive what they deserve. They have hurt us and we want to see them pay for it.

When we are angry in a godly way, we resist evil and its perpetrators; but we do not long for the offenders to "get what they deserve." Instead, we will prize reconciliation (Eph. 4:26) or restoration.

With these three distinctions in mind, we can see why most anger is sin. There are relatively few occasions when we experience true righteous indignation toward our children. Even when we are angry because they have disobeyed, we need to check our real reason for being distressed. Is the anger self-centered or is it lovingly based? We need to face the fact that carnal anger has a negative effect on our children and that it also constricts communication.

Yet we know that anger is "normal" in parenting. What can be done to overcome it? Although this is not the place for an in-depth treatment of the subject, we can suggest a few guidelines for handling our hostility so that it will not be destructive.

Resolving Parental Anger

It is, of course, one thing to recognize the destructiveness of anger and quite another to overcome the temptation to communicate in anger. The starting point is to become sensitive to the presence of anger and honestly acknowledge it. Not until we realize that our sharp voice, nagging, arguing, or outbursts are detrimental forms of anger can we begin to guard against these enemies of positive communication. Tied in with an awareness of anger is the recognition that any anger other than righteous indignation is sinful whether it is expressed or repressed. According to Scripture, the essence of sin resides in inner attitudes rather than overt actions. Jesus says, for example:

> "You have heard that it was said to the people long ago, 'Do not murder, and anyone who murders will be subject to judgment.' But I tell you that anyone who is angry with his brother will be subject to judgment. Again, anyone who says to his brother, 'Raca,' is answerable to the Sanhedrin. But anyone who says, 'You fool!' will be in danger of the fire of hell." (Matt. 5:21-22)

While there are pragmatic differences between bottling up anger and explosively releasing it, both are hurtful and both are considered sin by God. The repression of anger that generates depression, worry, anxiety, or any other malady is probably just as destructive of relationships and personal growth as are angry blasts.

Second, an awareness of our anger must be followed by restraint. Recognizing that we may not entirely eliminate sinful anger, we can still strive to prevent overreactions and to check impulses. Scripture challenges us:

> A fool gives full vent to his anger,
> but a wise man keeps himself under control.
> (Prov. 29:11)

While we are not to deny our anger, neither are we to give it free reign. By checking that first impulse to lash out we will dissipate a good deal of pressure and allow ourselves time for more loving actions.

A third guideline for handling anger is to understand its causes. Many of us are bewildered by our anger toward our children. We know it causes harm, but we have no insight into what triggers our frustration. While some may need the help of others to uncover the deep roots of anger, healing understanding often comes by asking a few questions. Did fatigue and tension trigger my hostility? Am I threatened when my child questions my authority? Was I looking for a scapegoat? Was I upset because our children reminded me of myself when I was younger? Is their behavior making me look like a poor parent? Does our children's stubbornness bring out my own? Probing the reasons for our excessive reactions may help free us from their power.

Once we have traced the causes of our anger we are ready for the fourth guideline: apply biblical principles to its resolution. When we see that anger is partially a defensive response to what we see as an attack on our self-esteem, for example, we can turn our attention to building a more biblical attitude toward ourselves. As we begin to see the sense of confidence, security, and worth that God offers to us we become less threatened by other's actions and consequently less likely to react in anger. And when we realize that our failures as parents have already been forgiven by God we can operate without the guilt that often stimulates anger.

A fifth guide for handling anger is to discharge unresolved hostilities in responsible ways. That is, if we need to "explode," we can ventilate it before a neutral party. When we do express our anger to our children, we should never say, "You make me angry!" This is an accusing statement that puts the blame for *our* anger on our *children!* A more accurate and helpful statement is: "I am very angry right now. Give me a little time and I'll try to talk this over fairly with you." By accepting responsibility for our own anger, we break the vicious cycle of blaming others. It is a very weighty experience for children to be blamed for their parents' anger. In fact, this confusing reversal of responsibility is at the core of much serious depression that occurs later in life.

A sixth principle for resolving anger is to apologize or ask forgiveness when we have attacked others or turned on them in anger. Christ said:

> "Therefore, if you are offering your gift at the altar and there remember that your brother has something against you, leave your gift there in front of the altar. First go and be reconciled to your brother; then come and offer your gift." (Matt. 5:23-24)

An honest confession of our offenses against our children helps remove the barriers our hostility has erected and sets the stage for them to be equally honest and repentant with us. A final help in handling our hostility is to recognize the sovereignty of God. At its core, anger is a rejection of God's sovereignty. It says, "God, I am not content with the way You permit me to be treated, and I demand that it be changed. Either the situation must change or those who are upsetting me must be punished. And I'll do it if You won't!" Christians who are learning to accept the reality of God's loving sovereignty and man's finiteness find it increasingly easy to give up the desire for revenge or the desire to demand their rights. Such persons leave matters in God's hands while learning to respond to their children in a loving, corrective manner that reflects the grace of God. This does not mean we sit back and do nothing. We continue to train our children and relate to others, but we give up the demand for revenge and retaliation.

Summary

The constructive handling of parental anger is one of the biggest keys to improving parent-child communication. When we are angry we are not reaching out in loving care of our children. Once we have learned to resolve our own resentments we can place ourselves in our children's shoes, listen with deep empathy, and respond with a sensitivity that communicates our understanding.

-12-

SEX EDUCATION IN THE HOME

The history of Christian thought on the subject of sexuality is a long, dark journey. The story, while at best intriguing, at worst is downright dismal. Contemporary young minds must find it incredible. Prior to the beginning of our own century it cannot be termed in any true sense positive.

With these words Dwight Small[1] begins a review of the views of sexuality held for the past nineteen centuries in the Christian church. Not until the twentieth century, he contends, did we begin to develop a positive and truly biblical conception of human sexuality.

Augustine believed that erotic desire in sexual intercourse was part of original sin. He said the true Christian "would prefer to beget children without this kind of lust."[2] Thomas Aquinas taught that intercourse was only for the purpose of procreation. And Martin Luther said, "Had God consulted me about it, I should have advised Him to continue the generation of the species by fashioning human beings out of clay, as Adam was made."[3]

With this heritage, it is little wonder that the process of educating children about sexuality still stirs anxiety in many Christian parents. In spite of our sophisticated and sex-oriented society, most parents feel a twinge of anxiety or embarrassment when their children ask about sex. Fortunately, in recent years we have seen some major improvements in the church's attitude toward sexuality. The sexual revolution of the past three decades, for all its negative influence, has brought human sexuality to the forefront and has forced the church to do some new thinking about this basic element of human relations. And out of this new study a more positive picture is developing—a picture that was part of Scripture but often went essentially unnoticed until this day.

The study of the Song of Solomon is a good case in point. In this beautiful Song a lover and his beloved describe their love for one another and how this love grows during their marriage. Although this Song is filled with descriptive detail about human love and sexuality, it has traditionally been interpreted as an allegory of God's spiritual relationship to His people. One noted commentary supports the suggestion that if the Song of Solomon were describing merely human love "it would have been positively objectionable, and never would have been inserted in the holy canon."[4] Early church fathers tell us that the Jews forbade anyone less than thirty years of age to read it. Some Jewish rabbis suggested that verse thirteen of chapter one ("My lover is to me a sachet of myrrh resting between my breasts") actually refers to the Shekinah glory between the two cherubim that stood over the ark in the Tabernacle! And a Christian scholar has contended that this pouch of myrrh between the woman's breasts refers to Christ appearing during the intertestamentary period![5] In commenting on these attempts to remove the plain sense of the Song as a human love story, J. Sidlow Baxter writes:

> To read some of the absurd and fanciful expositions associated with this theory, such as that the hair of the bride represents the mass of the nations converted to Christianity, is too much for a God-given sense of humor, and brings the whole theory into disrepute.[6]

Rejecting attempts to treat the Song of Solomon as merely allegory, Joseph Dillow has written on the subject of sexuality by dealing with this description of the love between Solomon and the Shulammite woman. He writes: "We want to . . . take a close look at God's guidelines for sex, love and marriage."[7]

David Hubbard sees neither allegory nor type in the Song of Solomon:

> It serves as an object lesson, an extended *māšāl*, illustrating the rich wonders of human love. As biblical teaching concerning physical love has been emancipated from sub-Christian asceticism, the beauty and purity of marital love have been more fully appreciated. The Song, though expressed in language too bold for western taste, provides a wholesome balance between the extremes of sexual excess or perversion and an ascetic denial of the essential goodness of physical love.[8]

Baxter gives us one of the most balanced perspectives on the nature and intent of this book of the Bible. He suggests:

> A true interpretation of the poem, therefore, will recognize in it a duality in unity, for while it is primarily the expression of "pure marital love as ordained by God in creation, and the vindication of that love as against both asceticism and lust," the deeper and larger meaning has reference to the heavenly Lover and His bride, the church.[9]

In other words, the Song of Solomon has both a natural-historical and an allegorical meaning.[10] But it has taken centuries to come to the point of looking at this book for practical insight into the nature of love and intimacy in marriage. Happily (as the recent surge of Christian publications on sexuality testifies),[11] this is now changing and we see a clear and positive biblical view of sex emerging. Without going into great detail we can summarize this new understanding of human sexuality in an eightfold manner:

1. Sex is God's creation and therefore innately good (Gen. 1:27).
2. Sex is an aspect of the full unity of male and female that God intended when He created Eve (Gen. 2:24; Mark 10:8).

3. Marital unity (including sex) is representative of the union of Christ and His bride, the church (Eph. 5:22-33).
4. Sex is designed partly for procreation (Gen. 1:28).
5. Sex is designed partly for communication (Gen. 4:1 KJV).
6. Sex is designed partly for pleasure (Prov. 5:18-19).
7. Sex outside of marriage is destructive (Exod. 20:14; Gal. 5:19-21).
8. A devout Christian life and good sexual adjustment should be mutually complementary (Heb. 13:4).

With this summary of biblical views on sexuality, we turn to the matter of sex education for children. The beginning point for positive sex education is a wholesome attitude on our part toward our own bodies and our sexuality. Not until we have accepted the beauty and rightness of our own sexuality can we communicate positive attitudes and insights on the subject to our children. This is the first of five specific guidelines for us to follow in educating our children about sex.

First, then, is an open and honest attitude toward the body and human sexuality. As a model parent, God sets a beautiful example in the Scriptures. The Bible "pulls no punches" when it comes to sex. It is forthright and explicit, not snide nor ashamed. Consider a few verses from the Song of Solomon:

How beautiful your sandaled feet,
O prince's daughter!
Your graceful legs are like jewels,
the work of a craftsman's hands.
Your navel is a rounded goblet
that never lacks blended wine.
Your waist is a mound of wheat
encircled by lilies.
Your breasts are like two fawns,
twins of a gazelle.
Your neck is like an ivory tower.
Your eyes are the pools of Heshbon
by the gate of Bath Rabbim.
Your nose is like the tower of Lebanon
looking toward Damascus.

Your head crowns you like Mount Carmel.
Your hair is like royal tapestry;
the king is held captive by its tresses.
How beautiful you are and how pleasing,
O love, with your delights!
Your stature is like that of the palm,
and your breasts like clusters of fruit.
I said, "I will climb the palm tree;
I will take hold of its fruit."
May your breasts be like the clusters of the vine,
the fragrance of your breath like apples,
and your mouth like the best wine.
(Song of Sol. 7:1-9)

Solomon adores his wife's body from head to toe: feet, legs, navel,[12] waist, breasts, neck, eyes, nose, head, and hair. We see no hint of embarrassment, guilt, or shame in Solomon and the Shulammite woman. Similarly, God apparently does not hesitate to discuss openly the intimacies of lovemaking with His children.

The first thing we need to understand about sex education is that we do not need to be embarrassed or hesitant to discuss the details of sexuality. We have no need to "hem and haw" when our children ask questions. We should talk about the parts of the body that relate to sexuality and discuss their function. We should be familiar with the processes of conception, pregnancy, and birth and speak freely to our children about them.

A second element in sex education is a positive parental example. In Ephesians 5:23-33 we read that Christ, as the head of the church, serves as a model for earthly husbands and wives. Christ's relationship to His bride is characterized by love, sacrifice, and faithfulness. In this relationship He typifies three of the key ingredients in biblical marriages. Parents, in living out this type of commitment, likewise model the ingredients of love relations to their children.

Although the various expressions of love, sacrifice, and faithfulness are frequently not considered a part of sexuality, they actually comprise essential ingredients of a biblical sexuality. Healthy sexual adjustment requires an understanding of the total relationship between men and women; therefore our children are significantly affected by our attitudes and actions in these areas. Love, sacrifice, and faithfulness provide an important emotional and spiritual bond for the physical side of sex.

Another part of the positive parental example that deserves special attention is the relationship between our sex-role adjustment and our child's developing view of sexuality. A boy needs a good relationship with both his father and mother to grow up with healthy attitudes about sex. One cause of sex-role confusion and homosexuality in today's society is the frequent absence of a male model in the home. Every boy needs a father who understands his needs, provides leadership, spends enjoyable times with him, and in general provides a good example of what a boy can grow up to be. Every boy also needs a mother who is happy with herself and her role in life. He needs a mother who loves him without overprotecting him and who encourages accomplishment without making excessive demands. A weak or broken relationship with either parent blurs a boy's masculinity. To illustrate, the combination of a domineering or overindulgent mother and a passive, weak father is one of the most frequent causes of male homosexuality. The father's weakness leaves the male child without a model of masculinity, while the mother's overinvolvement in the boy's life ties him to her and prevents him from moving away and establishing his own autonomy.

The same is true for a girl's sexual adjustment. A mother with strong resentment toward men will undoubtedly communicate this to her daughter, causing the girl to view men as weak, irresponsible, harsh, disinterested, or whatever else the mother believed them to be. Unconsciously the daughter projects this disabling quality on her own husband, hindering their emotional and sexual adjustment.

In the same way, a boy whose father depicts women as inferior, unintellectual, domineering, and so forth, will carry some of these attitudes into marriage. He will respond to his wife somewhat as his father did to his mother. This is the reason for saying that sex education is more than giving information. The main ingredients in sexual adjustment are healthy attitudes toward ourselves, our parents, and members of the opposite sex. If a woman mistrusts men or if a man believes women are objects to be used, no amount of knowledge about the physiology of sex will produce a rewarding sexual relationship. But a married couple with positive attitudes toward themselves and others should not have much difficulty with the physical side of sexuality.

If we follow God's example as a model parent we are led to a third principle of sex education: biblical sex education includes guidelines, instructions, and prohibitions. Consider the following passages:

> "You shall not commit adultery." (Exod. 20:14)

> No Israelite man or woman is to become a temple prostitute. You must not bring the earnings of a female prostitute or of a male prostitute into the house of the LORD your God to pay any vow, because the LORD your God detests them both. (Deut. 23:17-18)

> The acts of the sinful nature are obvious: sexual immorality, impurity and debauchery; idolatry and witchcraft; hatred, discord, jealousy, fits of rage, selfish ambition, dissensions, factions and envy; drunkenness, orgies and the like. I warn you, as I did before, that those who live like this will not inherit the kingdom of God. (Gal. 5:19-21)

God clearly instructs His children to "flee the evil desires of youth" (2 Tim. 2:22) and to avoid adultery and impurity. He also warns against sexual abuse in Proverbs 6:23-29.

In these passages youth are specifically instructed to follow their parents' teaching regarding sexual activity outside of marriage. We will not hesitate to teach our children that sexual intercourse outside of marriage is a sin. At the same time we will not build negative attitudes toward sexuality in general.

Often parents who suffer from guilt or anxiety over sex show a strong aversion to nudity and sexuality in general. This attitude is easily interpreted by children to mean that all sex is wicked and distasteful. Prohibition of sexual activity must be clearly connected with sex outside of the marriage commitment. Excessive focus on the sinfulness of misused sex communicates a most unhealthy attitude to the child. Even when this is occasionally punctuated with a statement to the effect that sex is "beautiful in marriage," the major message the child receives is that sex is wrong.

Calm talks with a child about appropriate clothing and respectable dating behavior can avoid the implication that sex is dirty or sinful and can foster the development of positive attitudes toward oneself and sexuality. When people have heard for years that sex is wrong, it is very difficult for them to marry and suddenly accept sex as good. While they may know intellectually that sex is good, years of hearing otherwise make it difficult to throw off the fear and guilt and secrecy of sex.

A fourth important principle in sex education is that God freely forgives sexual wrongdoing as well as other sins. Because of the anxiety and guilt that many experience due to the fact that they are sexual beings, there is a tendency to make sexual sin seem especially evil and perhaps even unforgivable. A Christian known to be guilty of sexual wrongdoing may even be branded for life. Sexual sins do have deep and far-ranging consequences, but we must beware of the Pharisee mentality.

> The teachers of the law and the Pharisees brought in a woman caught in adultery. They made her stand before the group and said to Jesus, "Teacher, this woman was caught in the act of adultery. In the law Moses commanded us to stone such women. Now what do you say?" They were using this question as a trap, in order to have a basis for accusing him.
>
> But Jesus bent down and started to write on the ground with his finger. When they kept on questioning him, he straightened up and said to them, "If any one of you is without sin, let him be the first to throw a stone at her." Again he stooped down and wrote on the ground.

At this, those who heard began to go away one at a
time, the older ones first, until only Jesus was left, with
the woman still standing there. Jesus straightened up
and asked her, "Woman, where are they? Has no one
condemned you?"

"No one, sir," she said.

"Then neither do I condemn you," Jesus declared.
"Go now and leave your life of sin."

(John 8:3-11)

The scribes and Pharisees singled out this woman in the
hope of trapping Jesus with their questions. But he turned the
tables on them and exposed their own guilt. Jesus said He
wouldn't condemn her to death for adultery, rather He told
her to sin no more. Sexual sins are compared with spiritual
idolatry in the Old Testament, but God forgives and forgets
them just like any other sin. They have all been paid for by
Christ, and our children need to know that God will grant full
forgiveness.

Perhaps the most important principle is that sex education
should be a normal part of daily living.[13] If we relegate it to
specific times or to books and lectures, we misunderstand our
task. Sex education isn't a lecture or a few bits of information.
It's a way of life. Just as information about sex and attitudes
toward sex are woven throughout Scripture, our children's sex
education should unfold naturally in our daily interaction with
them.

-13-

ACCOUNTABILITY: PARENT AND CHILD

High on the list of parent concerns—especially parents of adolescents and young adults—is the issue of personal responsibility or accountability. When a child rebels spiritually or develops other serious problems, whose fault is it? The child's? The parents'? Or is some other influence in society the culprit? These questions are of practical importance because the inescapable matter of responsibility profoundly affects our understanding of our role as parents and our understanding of our children.

We tend to go to one of two extremes on the issue of accountability. Some of us attempt to place all the responsibility on our children. We blame our children when they make an error and make it clear that "we have done the best we can." Others of us blame ourselves for our children's troubles. We frantically read every book available on rearing children, and on each page we find more mistakes that we unwittingly made. We feel like total failures and constantly berate ourselves for our children's problems.

Those of us who are in the latter group are suffering from excessive guilt and self-rejection. We feel a persistent need to blame and condemn ourselves, and this situation probably existed long before our children came on the scene. What is not initially so apparent, however, is that those of us who try to cast all responsibility on our children are also struggling with the same guilt problems. If we admit responsibility for our children's failures, we might be overcome with feelings of guilt and failure. So, instead, we place all the blame on our children. As one mother of a rebellious young adult said to me, "I couldn't admit I was to blame for my daughter's problems. If I did I would feel terrible!"

According to Scripture, both parents and children have responsibility for the child's behavior.

Parental Responsibility

One of the clearest and best-known illustrations of parental responsibility is the story of Eli and his sons, Hophni and Phinehas, recorded in the second chapter of First Samuel. Eli's sons were extremely sinful. They were showing contempt for the offerings the Israelites were sacrificing to God, and they were having intercourse with the women who worked at the entrance to the tabernacle. Eli, then an old man, attempted to correct his sons, but only mildly.

In chapter 3 of First Samuel the Lord revealed to Samuel that judgment would come on Eli and his family. The reason God had to intervene in Eli's family was because Eli failed to correct his wayward sons. God clearly put a major portion of the responsibility on Eli when he said, "For I told him that I would judge his family forever because of the sin he knew about; his sons made themselves contemptible, and he failed to restrain them" (1 Sam. 3:13).

In Exodus we find two more passages that speak to the responsibility of parents for their children's sins.

> "You shall not make for yourself an idol, or any likeness of what is in heaven above or on the earth beneath or in the water under the earth. You shall not worship them or serve them; for I, the LORD your God, am a jealous God, visiting the iniquity of the fathers on the children, on the third and fourth generations of those who hate me." (Exod. 20:4-6 NASB)

"[The LORD] will by no means leave the guilty unpunished, visiting the iniquity of fathers on the children and
the grandchildren to the third and fourth generations."
(Exod. 34:7 NASB)

Here we are told that the sins of parents carry into the third
and fourth generation. Not only does the Bible teach that our
sins influence our children, but also our grandchildren and
our great-grandchildren. Once again, we have several clear
biblical illustrations of this truth. One of the most potent is
found in the life of Abraham and his descendants.

Abraham was a man of great faith and was deeply loved by
God. Yet he set in motion a sinful pattern that lasted at least
three generations. Abraham had a habit of lying.

Now there was a famine in the land, and Abram went
down to Egypt to live there for a while because the
famine was severe. As he was about to enter Egypt, he
said to his wife Sarai, "I know what a beautiful woman
you are. When the Egyptians see you, they will say,
'This is his wife.' Then they will kill me but will let you
live. Say you are my sister, so that I will be treated well
for your sake and my life will be spared because of you."
(Gen. 12:10-13)

We read of the same thing later in the Book of Genesis.

Now Abraham moved on . . . into the region of the
Negev, and lived between Kadesh and Shur. For a while
he stayed in Gerar, and there Abraham said of his wife
Sarah, "She is my sister." (Gen. 20:1-2)

In Genesis 26 we find that Abraham's sin of lying was
picked up by his son. In fact, Isaac uses exactly the same story
his father told many years before.

So Isaac stayed in Gerar. When the men of that place
asked him about his wife, he said, "She is my sister,"
because he was afraid to say, "She is my wife." He
thought, "The men of this place might kill me on account
of Rebekah, because she is beautiful." (Gen. 26:6-7)

But Abraham's lying didn't end with the second generation.
Isaac and Rebekah had twin sons, Jacob and Esau. Jacob,

whose name means "supplanter," used deception on his blind father. When it was time for Isaac to pronounce a patriarchal blessing on Esau, Jacob and his mother Rebekah conspired together.

> Then Rebekah took the best clothes of Esau her older son, which she had in the house, and put them on her younger son Jacob. She also covered his hands and the smooth part of his neck with the goatskins. Then she handed to her son Jacob the tasty food and the bread she had made. He went to his father and said, "My father." "Yes, my son," he answered. "Who is it?" Jacob said to his father, "I am Esau, your firstborn." (Gen. 27:15-19)

The sin of deception practiced by Abraham powerfully affected the life of his grandson Jacob. In one form or another, the sins of the fathers have an effect on the third and fourth generations.

Abraham is not the only biblical example of this truth. The life of David bears out this same pattern. David, in spite of being Israel's greatest king, was guilty of several blatant offenses and apparently was not an effective father. As with Abraham, we can trace the results of David's sins through successive generations.

In addition to committing adultery with Bathsheba and arranging the murder of her husband Uriah (2 Sam. 11), David delivered seven of Saul's descendants to the Gibeonites to be murdered (2 Sam. 21:1-14). True to the judgment of the Lord spoken through Nathan the prophet (2 Sam. 12:7-12), conflict never left the house of David.

Amnon, David's son by Ahinoam, raped his half-sister Tamar (2 Sam. 13:1-22). In retribution, Amnon was murdered by Tamar's brother Absalom (2 Sam. 13:23-36), who then fled from David. Absalom later led a revolt against David (2 Sam. 15:1-23) and chased him from Jerusalem. Eventually Absalom was slain by David's general, Joab (2 Sam. 18:9-18).

Even Solomon, the son of David and Bathsheba and the last great king of Israel, spent his last years in shame. Like his father, Solomon had a problem with women. His wives and concubines numbered over one thousand (1 Kings 11:3), including foreign women for whom he built places of worship to false gods to satisfy their heathen beliefs (1 Kings 11:7-8). The family histories of many Old Testament stalwarts give pathetic testimony to individuals who were successful in leadership and religious service yet who were miserable failures at home. Our sinful patterns may not show up in our work—even our Christian work—but they will show up in our children and grandchildren. This is a sober warning to Christian parents and one that, if it were not for the grace of God, would be most discouraging. But the very passages that announce the persistence of sins to the third and fourth generations proclaim the all-encompassing grace of God.

> . . . but showing lovingkindness to thousands, to those who love Me and keep My commandments. (Exod. 20:6 NASB)

> . . . who keeps lovingkindness for thousands, who forgives iniquity, transgression and sin. (Exod. 34:7 NASB)

Charles Swindoll describes the grace that balances the "visiting of sins to the third and fourth generations." He writes:

> At first glance, this appears to be an awfully severe verse of Scripture. When I first began to study it, I thought, "How vengeful of God to do such a thing . . . how unfair!" And yet quite the opposite is true. He could have visited that same perversion, that distortion or bent, throughout the *entire* family history. Ultimately that would result in the very annihilation of mankind. But He says, "No, it will be visited until the third and fourth generations."

> Notice in verses 6 and 7 that the context is God's kindness and compassion. "The Lord God, compassionate, gracious, slow to anger, and abounding in lovingkindness and truth . . ." He keeps lovingkindness for thousands. He forgives iniquity and transgression and sin.[1]

The life of Timothy is a good example of the positive influence of godly parents and grandparents. In writing to young Timothy Paul says:

> I have been reminded of your sincere faith, which first
> lived in your grandmother Lois and in your mother
> Eunice and, I am persuaded, now lives in you also.
> (2 Tim. 1:5)

Timothy's faith was the result of the life and teaching of two
previous generations. Both his mother Eunice and his grandmother Lois were known for their faith and passed it on
through successive generations.

Children's Responsibility

Just as the Scripture teaches the responsibility of parents, it
also reveals that all people shoulder a personal responsibility
for their actions. Consider a few scriptural statements about
personal responsibility for sin.

> We all, like sheep, have gone astray,
>   each of us has turned to his own way;
> and the Lord has laid on him
>   the iniquity of us all.
>   (Isa. 53:6)

> The soul who sins is the one who will die. The son will
> not share the guilt of the father, nor will the father share
> the guilt of the son. The righteousness of the righteous
> man will be credited to him, and the wickedness of the
> wicked will be charged against him. (Ezek. 18:20)

> For the wages of sin is death, but the gift of God is
> eternal life in Christ Jesus our Lord. (Rom. 6:23)

God would be unjust in punishing sin if we were not personally responsible for our actions. The fact that we bear a
great responsibility for our children does not erase the fact
that our children also have a say in their own destiny. Scripture speaks specifically to the responsibility of children.

> Even a child is known by his actions,
>   by whether his conduct is pure and right.
>   (Prov. 20:11)

> Children, obey your parents in the Lord, for this is right.
> (Eph. 6:1)

Adam and Eve's first sin is a good example of personal responsibility. They could not "blame it on their parents"! But they did immediately try to shift responsibility away from themselves. Adam said, "The woman you put here with me—she gave me some fruit from the tree, and I ate it" (Gen. 3:12). And Eve said, "The serpent deceived me, and I ate" (Gen. 3:13).

Shared Responsibility

In the disobedience of Adam and Eve we see a case of shared responsibility for sin (Gen. 3:14-19). God tells us that Satan, speaking through the serpent, was partially responsible for Adam and Eve's sin and that he had to suffer for it (Gen. 3:14-15). Eve was partially responsible, and she had to suffer for it (Gen. 3:16). And Adam was partially responsible, and he had to suffer for his role (Gen. 3:17-19).

That both parent and child bear a share of the responsibility follows logically from the fact that both parent and child are sinners and are moral beings. Each party, however, shares a different aspect of responsibility. We are instructed to provide for our children's needs and train them properly. Children, in turn, are responsible for following our leadership and accepting increasing personal responsibility as they mature.

If we look again to God as our model parent, we gain another insight into the problem of responsibility. Paul promised: "And my God will meet all your needs according to his glorious riches in Christ Jesus" (Phil. 4:19).

Why is it that God can require obedience and righteousness from His children? Is it not in large measure because He *first* supplies our needs? As our heavenly Father, God reaches out to us, makes provisions for our physical, spiritual, and emotional needs and *then* expects us to respond. It would be totally unfair for God to require anything of us if He had not first provided sufficiently so that we could live up to His expectations.

We should do the same. We cannot justifiably expect obedience and maturity from our children unless we first fulfill their needs. An illustration may clarify this. Let's suppose the father of a teen-age girl is rarely home. When he is, he is too busy to be lovingly involved in his daughter's life. He may also be critical and judgmental and not supportive of her friends. Her mother is also extremely busy, or perhaps she is prone toward depression. She isn't really happy in her role of wife and mother and finds it difficult to participate in her daughter's world. On top of this the parents are quite restrictive, and there is a great deal of tension and hostility in the home.

After years in this environment, the girl reaches adolescence with major unmet needs. She does not feel loved and accepted by her father. She lacks a sense of pride in her femininity. She has a serious lack of self-confidence and worth. She also harbors a great deal of anger and resentment toward her parents.

When this girl begins to date, she will bring all of this background of resentment and unfulfilled needs to her new relationships. She may withdraw for fear of further rejection. Or she may get deeply involved with the first boy she begins to date. When sexual temptations come, she will probably be more susceptible than if she had a more positive family life. In her search to fill previously unmet needs she is more likely to become sexually promiscuous. Since she doesn't feel loved by the most important man in her life she will do rash things to gain a temporary sense of love or satisfaction.

Obviously this girl bears a responsibility for her actions. She could have responded to her parents' rejection of her differently. At the same time, however, the parents have clearly failed to meet her needs. If they had been more adequate suppliers of the girl's needs, ·she would still have faced temptations. She would still have had to cope with her awakening sexual desires, her need to be loved, her adolescent curiosity, and whatever peer pressure might exist. But she would not have had the extra burden of negative attitudes toward herself, deep unmet needs for love, and desires to rebel against her parents. These additional factors, the direct result of her parents' failures, may well have been "the straw that broke the camel's back." They added an almost unbearable pressure to give in to temptation.

Responsibility and Grace

One reason so many people are deeply troubled by the issue of responsibility is their unresolved sense of guilt. Guilt always seeks a scapegoat. Grace, however, desires to pull together for the future. Once a parent or a child has come to grip with his own sinfulness and God's forgiveness, the strained issue of responsibility begins to fade into the background. We no longer need to blame our children because we can freely acknowledge our responsibility and accept divine forgiveness. Until both parents and children perceive and appropriate God's grace and His forgiveness, they will smolder or argue endlessly about who is to blame—and the failures will proliferate. Accepting responsibility allows everyone concerned to stop blaming others and begin taking steps toward improvement.

-14-

ΦARENTS AND THE EXPERTS

In the last thirteen chapters we have taken a scriptural look at the major aspects of rearing children. Throughout these chapters we have commented on a number of less than biblical approaches to parenting. We have not, however, attempted to present a system for evaluating the vast array of books and materials available to parents. Yet both the sheer number of these books and their frequently conflicting advice point to the need for some way of selecting among all the available books and knowing how to study them discerningly. As we have seen, even Christian authors take widely opposing views on some very significant aspects of parenting. In fact, the lack of consensus is almost startling. One pamphlet (quoted earlier) purporting to give a biblical view of discipline has this to say about spanking:

> My obedience to God to train my child requires that every time I ask him to do something, whatever it is, I must see that he obeys. When I have said it once in a normal tone, if he does not obey immediately, I must take up my switch and correct him enough to hurt so he will not want it repeated.[1]

On the same topic Howard Hendricks writes:

There are too many people running around with a biblical two by four who really don't know very much of what the Scriptures teach regarding discipline.[2]

Speaking of ways to motivate children, C. S. Lovett writes:

If I were to ask, "Which emotion should fathers and mothers use to counter Satan's appeals?" you'd come back with the sweet reply—"LOVE." That sounds very nice and proper, doesn't it? Well, I'm sorry—that's NOT the emotion. We need something more powerful than parental love. There's only one emotion that is greater—FEAR. I know that startles you. But mama-love and papa-love do not have the same effect on them it used to.

Parents, seeking to compete with Satan, must answer with the countering emotion of fear. Fear is the one great emotion to which everyone responds. Fear alone can check the awesome forces unleashed in teens.[3]

In contrast, another Christian author writes:

Genuine parental love, naturally demonstrated, comes nearer to being the "cure all" for all the problems of child care than anything else that one could possess. Your love as a parent is most important to your child at the very moment when he is least loveable.[4]

And on the topic of obedience, authority, and respect, James Dobson says:

First, the parent should decide whether an undesireable behavior represents a direct challenge to his authority—to his position as father or mother. Punishment should depend on that evaluation. . . . In my opinion, spankings should be reserved for the moment a child (age ten or less) expresses a defiant "I will not!" or "You shut up!" When a youngster tries this kind of stiff-necked rebellion, you had better take it out of him, and pain is a marvelous purifier. When nose-to-nose confrontation occurs between you and your child, it is not the time to have a discussion about the virtues of obedience. It is not the occasion to send him in his room to pout. It is not appropriate to wait until poor, tired old dad comes plodding in from work, just in time to handle the conflicts of the day. You have drawn a line in the dirt and the child has deliberately flopped his big, hairy toe across it. Who is going to win? Who has the most courage? Who is in charge here?[5]

In contrast, Lawrence Richards writes:

In the first place, obedience is an inadequate goal for the Christian to set. Both spiritual leaders in the church and Christian parents in the home must set as their goal a growing love for Christ that will issue in an individual's free choice to obey Him. . . . The concept of requiring response, so essential in the whole notion of secular authority, also must be questioned. One can "require" obedience. But no one can require an inner change.

It is true that as parents we can enforce certain behavior. During childhood this is an important part of guiding the growth of our child's personalities. But no one can force or coerce another to act willingly. In fact, the whole idea of coercion to require a particular action implies that the person being required is unwilling! If he chose to act willingly there would be no need to "require"!

So somehow, the Christian's use of authority is intrinsically different from that of the secular authority. Spiritual authority seeks to encourage a willing response—not to require a prescribed behavior.[6]

Needless to say, this kind of contradiction leaves the parent looking for Christian guidance in a predicament. Who is right? Who can be believed? Two authors, both Christians, take opposite views on basic aspects of child rearing. The solution obviously lies in testing the position of both authors against the Scriptures, but this is not an easy task. Both authors quote Scripture and presumably both are sincere. Although some differences of interpretation of Scripture are inevitable, I believe we can improve our assessment of the counsel of "experts" with the aid of discriminating guidelines. I recommend the following seven-fold method of evaluating the biblical accuracy of material for parents.

1. *We need to discern the author's attitude toward the Bible.* While books by non-Christians or Christians with a low view of Scripture may have excellent insights and helpful sug-

gestions, they lack a solid foundation for erecting a structure of child-rearing principles. If we are aware of an author's attitude toward Scripture, we can be sensitive to areas of potential strength and weakness in the writing. Does the author openly reject the authority and inspiration of the Bible? Does he flatly disagree with plain truths revealed in Scripture? Even though few secular authors would openly state this view (for fear of alienating Christian readers), many do think this way. They do not see the Bible as a positive source of child-rearing principles; many, in fact, believe that Christian concepts of sin, guilt, and authority foster neurotic fears, guilty consciences, and passive or rebellious children.

A step removed from total rejection of biblical authority are those who pick and choose which scriptural injunctions and illustrations are valid for today. They may applaud, for example, Jesus' attention to little children (Matt. 19:13-14) or His exaltation of love and forgiveness in the parable of the lost son (Luke 15:11-32) to support their view of rearing children. But the use of physical discipline or other scriptural practices may be summarily dismissed as outdated cultural accretions because they clash with the experts' opinions.

The desirable attitude, of course, is that an author accept the Bible's (and Christ's) full authority and accuracy. Before differences of interpretation can be fruitfully considered, a common acceptance of Scripture's own claims is important.

"Do not think that I have come to abolish the Law or the Prophets; I have not come to abolish them but to fulfill them. I tell you the truth, until heaven and earth disappear, not the smallest letter, not the least stroke of a pen, will by any means disappear from the Law until everything is accomplished. Anyone who breaks one of the least of these commandments and teaches others to do the same will be called least in the kingdom of heaven, but whoever practices and teaches these commands will be called great in the kingdom of heaven." (Matt. 5:17-19)

All Scripture is God-breathed and is useful for teaching, rebuking, correcting and training in righteousness, so that the man of God may be thoroughly equipped for every good work. (2 Tim. 3:16-17)

Above all, you must understand that no prophecy of Scripture came about by the prophet's own interpretation. For prophecy never had its origin in the will of man, but men spoke from God as they were carried along by the Holy Spirit. (2 Peter 1:20-21)

The Bible says that all of Scripture is (1) applicable to human lives, (2) given by God, and (3) without error.

As important as the author's attitude toward Scripture is, it is only the first criterion for conscientious Christian parents. Many authors are intellectually committed to the truth of Scripture, and yet they abuse biblical revelation.

2. *We must also look for consistency and comprehensiveness in the author's use of Scripture.* The biblical accuracy of a book cannot be measured by either the amount of Scripture it quotes or by the author's statement of belief in the Bible. Some authors make use of Scripture and confidently claim their book contains *the* biblical approach, yet they differ with authors who use equal amounts of Scripture and are equally committed to their approach! Rather than basing our confidence on the amount of Scripture an author uses, we need to base it on the manner in which Scripture is used. For example, does the author resort largely to a proof-texting approach and try to support beliefs from isolated verses? Or does the author evidence a grasp of the entirety of Scripture and interpret teachings within their divinely given context?

Some Christian authors have taken a verse or two of Scripture and claimed that Christians should never own insurance. Similarly, those who take a number of Scripture passages out of context and advocate the exclusive use of spanking or fear-oriented style of parenting are missing the mark of total biblical revelation—no matter how many verses they quote to support their ideas! Some authors impress readers with voluminous Scripture references and the unthinking reader can fall into the habit of assuming that these Scriptures are used in their proper context and in a manner consistent with the rest of biblical revelation. [7]

3. *Books on parenting must be checked for their view of human nature.* Here is the major weakness of most secular books on parenting and, unfortunately, of some Christian books. They tend to follow either the humanistic assumption that children are born essentially good or a behavioristic philosophy that fails to recognize the freedom, dignity, and worth of the human being. We have discussed the grave inadequacy of this humanistic approach earlier, but we should note that many books from this perspective contain excellent material on self-esteem and communication. Operating from the assumption that children are not innately sinful, they focus on the child's strengths, possibilities, and potentialities. They also stress the parents' need to provide a positive, nurturing home environment since they see children's adjustment problems coming almost solely (if not completely) from their environment. These books have excellent material on communication because they shun authoritarianism and emphasize the child's right to be heard and the importance of loving and honest communication in the family.[8]

Unfortunately, this humanistic focus on a child's strengths and possibilities fails to complete the picture and consequently denies another major aspect of human nature—sinfulness. For this reason books by humanistic authors tend to be relatively weak on the corrective aspects of discipline and training as well as on the constructive role of parental authority.

In the last two decades behavioristic psychology has won a dominant position in the social sciences. Arising first in the laboratories of experimental psychologists, it has been promoted by prominent educators, psychologists, and other behavioral scientists in almost every area of life—especially the educating and rearing of children. Many recent books for parents are built largely, if not entirely, on this foundation, and most school psychologists and educators are trained in behavioristic methods of controlling behavior.

In brief, behavioristic theory stresses environmental factors that "reward" a person's conduct and consequently "condition" the person to respond in a certain way. Giving little or no attention to experiences within the individual, behaviorism stresses the environmental forces that shape our lives. Christians take three positions toward this view. Some, such as Jay Adams, reject it out of hand because it contains unbiblical suppositions. Adams writes:

> When Dobson, for instance, recommends strictly behavioristic methods for child raising in the name of Christianity, he badly confuses important conditions and erases lines that forever must be drawn closely. His near-total capitulation to behaviorism is couched in Christian terms but really introduces an equally godless system into the Christian home while purporting to be a Christian reaction to permissiveness. In Dobson's methods there is no place for nouthetic confrontation. Reward and punishment are prominent (particularly the former) and the need for structure is emphasized. But Dobson's approach is cold and godless. It centers upon manipulation but says nothing of biblical confrontation.[9]

Few Christians would take such a strong stance against behaviorism (let alone call the approach in *Dare to Discipline* "cold and godless"). Yet some feel compelled to reject anything connected with behaviorism because of some of its underlying presuppositions.[10]

A second group goes to the opposite extreme and uncritically accepts behavioristic writings. They do not bother to think through the implications of behaviorism's view of the human being. But behaviorism holds a mixture of truth and error, and the wise parent will separate the two. Behaviorism has developed a number of demonstrated principles or facts. The fact that attitudes and actions that are rewarded are more likely to recur, for example, cannot legitimately be questioned. Even Scripture uses the concepts of reward and punishment. But the fact that conditioning does occur does not prove that *all* actions are determined by the reward system of our environment and that we therefore are not personally accountable for our deeds. Francis Schaeffer puts it this way:

It is important at this point to recognize what the Christian position is. The Christian position does not say there is no chemical or psychological conditioning. Some may argue that way, but they are trapped because chemical and psychological conditioning can be demonstrated. . . . But to a Christian, though man may undergo a good deal of conditioning, he is not only the product of conditioning. Man has a mind; he exists as an ego, an entity standing over against the machine—like part of his being.[11]

Christian parents, in my opinion, should keep four things in mind as they study books written from a behavioral perspective. The first is that they can gain a great deal of insight into the causes of children's misbehavior and into ways of altering behavior. Principles of reward and punishment do work![12] At the same time, Christian parents should be alert to the fact that as creations of God our children do have the freedom to make their own choices and set their own direction. Third, parents should realize that most behaviorists focus on a child's external behavior rather than on internal attitudes. While this has its place, Scripture gives priority to the attitudes of the heart.

"No good tree bears bad fruit, nor does a bad tree bear good fruit. Each tree is recognized by its own fruit. People do not pick figs from thornbushes, or grapes from briers. The good man brings good things out of the good stored up in his heart, and the evil man brings evil things out of the evil stored up in his heart. For out of the overflow of his heart his mouth speaks. (Luke 6:43-45)

In addition to shaping our children's attitudes and behavior through conditioning, we need to be building into their lives an abundance of love and respect, and we should not limit our concepts of discipline and training to rewards and related behavioral techniques.

A final caution about behaviorism is its weak foundation for self-esteem. Since secular behaviorists deny that people are created and see them only as a higher form of animal, they have no adequate foundation on which to build dignity and self-esteem. Although the principles of behaviorism can be used to reinforce positive self-evaluation, the underlying philosophical stance of radical behavioral philosophy leaves no effective starting place for self-esteem.[13]

As we saw in an earlier chapter, our attitude toward family government issues logically from our view of human nature. This prompts our fourth guideline for evaluating the adequacy of books for parents.

4. *Check the author's position on family government or leadership in order to determine whether the view is balanced.*

The two unacceptable extremes are the authoritarian approach, with its "children should be seen and not heard" philosophy, and the permissive approach, which shows disdain for restraint. Probably no author strikes a perfect balance of respect and discipline toward children even in theory, but readers can watch for clues that signal a sharp leaning in one direction or the other. Authoritarianism, found frequently among Christian authors, sets the parents up as gods, minimizes the significance of children, and shows little respect for them. It makes excessive use of parental power and emphasizes conformity and obedience more than inner maturity and growth. The permissive approach is just the opposite. In emphasizing the uniqueness of individuals and a deep respect for children they overlook the child's need for guidance, discipline, and correction.

Key words like *control, power, winning,* and phrases such as "showing a child who's boss" are indicators of authoritarian leanings. Coupled with the use of fear to produce obedience and the threat of anger on the part of the parent, these are signs of an overemphasis on control, parental power, and authoritarianism.

Permissive and democratic authors, on the contrary, steadfastly avoid or vehemently denounce the whole concept of authority. They usually reject the use of physical discipline, and they stress the innate goodness of children.

The biblical model stands between these extremes and emphasizes parental provision, loving leadership, deep respect for the child's worth and individuality, and an awareness of the child's need for training and correction. It contains genuine sensitivity to the child's needs and feelings, but also recognizes the place of authority and correction. The author who espouses these values represents the comprehensive biblical view of human nature and is a reliable teacher.

5. *Check the author's understanding of positive discipline.* As we saw in chapters 5, 6, and 7, child training and discipline involve a great deal more than corrective reactions to the child's misbehavior. Rightly conceived, discipline involves the entire process of child education, training, and correction. Any author who makes physical discipline the only or the major means of correction should be immediately suspect. The Bible does not teach that physical correction is the primary means of discipline or training. And authors who fail to see that correction is a loving process rather than a punitive one are blind to the biblical plan. Poor vision here leads to pitfalls further along.

6. *Measure the author's views on accountability.* Some authors try to blame all of children's problems and maladjustments on their sinful nature, and others place full responsibility on parents. Both of these views miss the mark of Scripture. Parents are responsible for supplying their children's needs and for lovingly instructing and correcting them, while children are responsible for following their parents' leadership and accepting an increasing responsibility for their own choices and direction. Both parties must bear responsibility in order for healthy development to take place.

7. *A final guide for evaluating the adequacy of parenting material is the author's sensitivity to the inner needs and struggles of parents and children alike.* Some authors focus so strongly on techniques for changing a child's behavior that they neglect the deep needs and feelings every child possesses. Others, in offering well-meaning advice, overlook the struggles that parents face. In pointing out where parents fail, they heap additional guilt on heavily burdened parents. Jesus, who cared about adults and children alike, was touched with

the feelings of our infirmities (Heb. 2:17-18; 4:14-18). In His compassion, understanding, kindness, and patience, He demonstrated the traits that inspire emulation. Parents who hope to keep enriching their relationships with their children will find the right help in authors who reflect this divine sensitivity rather than in those who emphasize techniques and strategy for outward conformity and performance.

The "experts" are human like everyone else, and no one hits that perfect ideal. In an area as important as child rearing we need to evaluate carefully our sources of guidance by the light of Scripture.

–1–

THE
ᏢARENTING
ᏢEVOLUTION

Good parents don't just happen! I know a few people who find it easy to be good parents. They are naturally cool, calm, and collected; so they hit it off well with their children. They are also sensitive and kind; yet they find it easy to carry out needed discipline. These parents enjoy their children and have few hassles with them. Even when the children encounter adolescence, things go smoothly between the two generations. These people seem to be naturally effective parents. Most of us, however, are not that way. We have had to work at parenting.

The following workbook exercises are intended to help in the task of becoming better parents; they will give you an opportunity to review the key points of each of the previous chapters as well as apply these concepts to your own family.

The exercises that follow are written so they can be used by parents in a study group or a class, as well as by couples in their own homes. Each chapter consists of several exercises that can be easily completed in less than an hour. If you decide to use this book in a study group, I suggest that you study one chapter during each meeting. If you go much faster than this, you probably will not have enough time to apply the principles to your family life. I would also suggest that whether you are using this book in your own home or in a group setting, complete no less than one chapter each month. We tend to forget what we have learned earlier and lose interest in a topic if we stay away from it too long.

Before we begin our study I would like to share three important suggestions that can make these exercises more helpful. Each of these suggestions relates to our feelings about ourselves as parents and to the way we approach the task of parenting.

Have Patience

There is a little song our children used to sing that goes like this:

> Have patience. Have patience.
> Don't be in such a hurry.
> When you get impatient,
> you only start to worry.
> Remember, remember,
> that God is patient too.
> And think of all the times when
> others have to wait on you.

This song ends with a reference to being patient with others, but these lines also apply to learning to be patient with ourselves. If you are like most parents you occasionally get "down" on yourself. There are times when nothing seems to go right—the children are fussy and sassy, they are fighting and they are disobedient. Reasoning with them works for about the first ten minutes. Then you correct them, but that's no more effective than reasoning. Finally, in utter exasperation, you blow your stack, let out a yell, and send them to their rooms. If you are a mother, you may let them know they are really going to get it when their dad comes home!

Once you get your wits about you, you wonder how things could be different. You want to learn effective ways of dealing with your children, but nothing seems to work. At this point you may turn to classes, books, or lectures on child discipline, and they are often helpful. But you sometimes come away with an even greater sense of guilt. You already knew you had some problems, but now you see how bad things really are!

This is depressing; and, what's more, it isn't necessary. One of the first prerequisites for becoming a better parent is to learn to be patient with yourself. You have spent twenty, thirty, or forty years becoming the person you are, and you will not be transformed overnight. If you expect too much too soon, you will only put yourself under a bigger pile of guilt and condemnation. And you will be so busy focusing on your failures that you will not be able to see your strengths and learn new ways of relating.

God does not expect any of us to be perfect. In fact, the Greek word translated "perfect" in the New Testament actually refers to maturity. It was used in Christ's day to refer to fully ripened fruit. And fruit doesn't ripen overnight. We, too, must go through seasons. Every parent starts out "green." We don't know the ropes. We have some natural parent instincts, but we also have a lot of habits and patterns we will have to change. We need the fertile soil of new insights if we are to learn to be more effective parents.

All of this takes time, for it is one thing to hear what we should or could be doing; and it is quite another to put it into practice. This book will help you practice biblical principles of child rearing. But don't be in a rush! God does not watch over us for the purpose of seeing whether we're perfect or not, and neither do our children expect perfection. You will learn much more quickly if you learn to "hang loose." It is a paradox that those who vow they are never going to react a certain way again are the ones most likely to fall back into an old pattern. We use so much energy trying to avoid the negatives that we don't have any left for doing what we want to do! When we realize we will never be perfect, we find it easier to forgive ourselves and our children and to keep moving in a positive direction.

One Step at a Time

For several years now I have been conducting seminars and training sessions for parents. After the first few seminars I learned a very important lesson. I told the participants to stop trying to change everything at once! Several people had reported to me the disaster that took place after they arrived home fresh from my seminar and tried to rearrange the whole family and put everything (and everyone) in order. It just doesn't work. It is too sudden and too much for everyone concerned.

Now, when I talk to parents, I suggest they take one thing at a time. Don't try to stop temper tantrums, sibling fights, mealtime problems, and curfew hassles all at once. Pick one problem, think it through carefully, and work it out. After that one has been resolved, then move on. That is the best way to grow.

This same principle applies to your study of this book. I have tried to communicate only one or two major ideas in each chapter. If I have communicated several ideas in any chapter, pick the one or two things that seem most important to you and focus your efforts there. You will learn much more in this way than by trying to put into practice every point in the entire book. After you have begun to apply one concept or one new way of responding to your children, then move on to another. If you try to go too quickly, none of the insights and principles will ever "soak in" enough to be of lasting value.

Going It Alone

Here is a third key to becoming a better parent: Find someone with whom you can regularly share your struggles as a parent. No matter how great our family life, we all have moments of frustration and despair. We get all caught up in old habits, or our children enter an especially difficult age or stage of development. When this happens, we need help. We need a friend to whom we can turn to relieve our frustration. And we need someone who can help us see what is happening and give us a new perspective.

This is why it is best to study this book with your spouse, or a friend, or a study group. Other people can often see with much greater clarity how we can best be helped. They can give us the encouragement and support we need. And they can allow us to help them. As a matter of fact, the best way to improve your parenting skills is to join a study group and have at least one discussion with a friend from the group between each meeting. If you can't get together in person, you can at least phone one another weekly to see how things are going. Give yourself time to discuss the previous or the upcoming lesson, to chat about things in general, and to see if there are any problems you can help each other with.

If You Are in a Study Group

Now let's assume you'd like to be in a study group. Your first thought may well be, *Who would be our leader?* Let me suggest that you might be the perfect person! You don't have to be an expert to lead these exercises. In fact, these chapters are not written to be "taught." They are intended to be studied and experienced. The readings and work-book assignments stand by themselves; so you don't need a set of lectures by a professional teacher. All you need is a desire to be a better parent, an ability to get along with others, and a willingness to do a little work. Then merely talk to a few friends; and if they're interested, you're on your way.

Here are some suggestions for the first meeting.[1] After that the basic pattern is established.

1. Begin by having the members introduce themselves and tell one unique or humorous quality about one of their children. It is also good to ask members why they came to the study group and what they hope to gain from it.

2. See that each person has a copy of this book.

3. List the topics to be covered at each meeting and assign the relevant chapters. I suggest that you follow the sequence of chapters used in this book because the order was established with a study group in mind.

4. Use approximately fifteen minutes of the meeting for reading chapter 2, "The Bible Speaks to Parents." It is not a lengthy chapter, and most people will read it within fifteen minutes; besides, this eliminates the need to lecture! After everyone has finished, take a few minutes to review the basic ideas. Then have everyone fill out exercise 1. This, too, should take no more than ten or fifteen minutes. In two simple steps you have involved everyone in the class activities. Sharing answers to exercise 1 is a good way to close the first session.

5. Arrange to phone each member once a week or have group members select a phone partner or phone couple. Phone partners contact each other every week, as discussed above. This phoning may seem to be a nuisance at first, but we have found it to be a key to the success of the course. It soon develops into a stimulating discussion of successes and failures in applying the study material, and close friendships may also evolve out of these discussions.

---

[1] This section is adapted from the author's *Guide to Child Rearing*, a parents' workbook for *Help! I'm a Parent*.

After the first session you are well on your way. The exercises carry the group along step by step, and the only input you need to give is to moderate the group or class discussions. Here are a few pointers for guiding these discussions.

1. Encourage everyone to participate by calling on the more quiet persons to share their answers. I often ask each person in the group to relate her or his answer to one of the exercises.

2. Encourage members to share specific examples of their successes and failures. The successes encourage others, and the failures provide an opportunity to clarify things when techniques are being misapplied.

3. Be positive and complimentary when members are sharing.

4. After someone describes an attempt to apply a new principle, ask others to evaluate whether it was successful. Encourage members to point out effective techniques and positive attitudes. Also see that they kindly but clearly mention weaknesses in the applications.

5. If one person tries to dominate the conversation, express thanks for the comments and then say something like, "Now, I'd like to know what Bill has tried."

6. Maintain the conviction that the Bible is the group's ultimate authority. Encourage members to share relevant Scripture passages and principles.

7. Use the first few minutes of each meeting to review briefly the major points of the previous lesson.

8. Use the next portion of each meeting to discuss attempts to apply the previous lesson's principles.

Here is a good chance to have each person share one experience.

9. If you decide not to present the new material in a lecture, simply make the reading assignment for the next meeting and close. If you meet for longer than one hour, it is often good to use twenty or thirty minutes at the close of each meeting for reading the next chapter and completing one of the workbook exercises. There are two reasons for this working ahead—first, most of us are busy, and, second, we don't read much. You may get some people to read more during that twenty or thirty minutes than they would during the rest of the entire week! When you introduce each new lesson in this way, you see that everyone gets started. The personal satisfaction that comes from beginning a new lesson encourages everyone to complete the work for the next meeting.

10. Establish the following principle: Anyone can share an experience or give an opinion on the part of the lesson being discussed so long as he or she has done the preliminaries of reading that part of the chapter and completing the workbook exercise. There are important reasons for this. First of all, some people like to talk excessively about their own ideas. The purpose of this class is to discuss and apply basic biblical principles, not to exchange pet peeves. By seeing to it that everyone who talks has read the material and completed the exercise, the tendency to stray is radically reduced. This restriction also indicates to the members the importance of applying the material, and it motivates them to do the work. Until your members do several of the exercises and see their value some may want to come to listen rather than to do.

THE ⑬IBLE
SPEAKS
TO ⑭ARENTS

The Bible is filled with insights and principles for rearing children. Unfortunately, many parents are unaware of these rich resources. Chapter 2 points out five biblical sources of advice and guidance for Christian parents:

- Specific commands and promises
- Teachings on God's relationship as heavenly Father to His earthly children
- Teachings on the nature of human personality, especially the twin facts of our creation in God's image and the results of sin in our lives and in the lives of our children
- Examples of family living in the Bible
- Counsel on relationships with others

The exercises in this chapter give examples of these five sources of truth for parents and then apply these rich scriptural resources to family living. In this way these exercises serve as an introduction to our major theme: we can find practical guidance for parenting in the Bible.

EXERCISE 1

Here are two biblical commands to parents. Read these verses and complete the questions below.

Fathers, do not exasperate your children; instead, bring them up in the training and instruction of the Lord. (Eph. 6:4)

Fathers, do not embitter your children or they will become discouraged. (Col. 3:21)

1. What do you think it means to "exasperate" and "embitter" a child?

_____

_____

_____

_____

2. Different translations and paraphrases of the Bible often shed new light on the meaning of a passage. Read the verses above in at least two other Bibles and insert below the wording that is most meaningful to you. (Be sure to include at least one of the following versions: The Amplified Bible, The Living Bible, or The New Testament in Modern English [Phillips].)

Ephesians 6:4 _____

_____

_____

_____

Colossians 3:21 _____

_____

_____

_____

3. Do you recall a time when you were exasperated with or bitter toward your parents? If so, describe your feelings at that time—how did you feel toward them? Toward yourself? Toward others involved? If you can't recall an instance involving your parents, think of one in which your spouse, an acquaintance, or an employer was the other party.

_____

_____

_____

_____

_____

_____

_____

_____

4. Describe a recent instance in which you exasperated or embittered one of your children. Write out (or discuss with your spouse or study group) what happened by telling what led up to the problem, the way you handled it, and your attitudes and actions as well as those of your child.

_____

_____

_____

_____

_____

_____

_____

5. In the future what can you do to avoid hassles like this or to get out of them without exasperating, embittering, or discouraging your child? Discuss.

_____

_____

_____

EXERCISE 2

The Bible describes God as our heavenly Father. In His relationship to us we find an illustration of perfect parenting. John writes:

> See how very much our heavenly Father loves us, for he allows us to be called his children—think of it— and we really are! But since most people don't know God, naturally they don't understand that we are his children. (1 John 3:1 LB)

A. The best known of all the psalms is probably Psalm 23. But have you ever read it while thinking of God as our model parent? Read this psalm and take special note of the things God does for us as our "shepherd" (or "father"). Then write down five things God does for us that we can also do for our children.*

> The LORD is my shepherd, I shall lack nothing.
>   He makes me lie down in green pastures,
> he leads me beside quiet waters,
>   he restores my soul.
> He guides me in paths of righteousness
>   for his name's sake.
> Even though I walk
>   through the valley of the shadow of death,
> I will fear no evil,
>   for you are with me
> your rod and your staff,
>   they comfort me.

*An asterisk within an exercise indicates that there is an answer key at the close of the chapter.

> You prepare a table before me
> in the presence of my enemies.
> You anoint my head with oil;
> my cup overflows.
> Surely goodness and love will follow me
> all the days of my life,
> and I will dwell in the house of the LORD
> forever.

1. _____

2. _____

3. _____

4. _____

5. _____

B. A few verses describing God's fatherly care and commitment to His children are given below. Read these verses and then jot down at least five things that are true of God's relationship with us that could also characterize our relationship with our children.*

> He led me to a place of safety, for he delights in me. (Ps. 18:19 LB)

> My God is changeless in his love for me and he will come and help me. He will let me see my wish come true upon my enemies. (Ps. 59:10 LB)

> Jehovah is kind and merciful, slow to get angry, full of love. He is good to everyone, and his compassion is intertwined with everything he does. (Ps. 145:8–9 LB)

> He is their shield, protecting them and guarding their pathway. (Prov. 2:8 LB)

> For long ago the Lord had said to Israel: I have loved you, O my people, with an everlasting love; with loving-kindness I have drawn you to me. (Jer. 31:3 LB)

> For I am convinced that nothing can ever separate us from his love. Death can't, and life can't. The angels won't, and all the powers of hell itself cannot keep God's love away. Our fears for today, our worries about tomorrow, or where we are—high above the

sky, or in the deepest ocean—nothing will ever be able to separate us from the love of God demonstrated by our Lord Jesus Christ when he died for us. (Rom. 8:38–39 LB)

1. _____

2. _____

3. _____

4. _____

5. _____

EXERCISE 3

Below are two passages that describe facets of the human personality. After reading these verses answer the questions below.*

What is man that you are mindful of him,
    the son of man that you care for him
You made him a little lower than the heavenly beings
    and crowned him with glory and honor.

You made him ruler over the works of your hands;
    you put everything under his feet:
all flocks and herds,
    and the beasts of the field,
the birds of the air,
    and the fish of the sea,
    all that swim the paths of the seas.

O LORD, our Lord,
    how majestic is your name in all the earth!
(Ps. 8:4–9)

We all, like sheep, have gone astray,
    each of us has turned to his own way;
and the LORD has laid on him
    the iniquity of us all.
(Isa. 53:6)

1. What two major truths about the human race are described in these passages?

   a. _____

   _____

   b. _____

   _____

2. List at least three implications of these two truths for our understanding of children and our relationship with them.

   Psalm 8:4–9 (Children as Image-bearers)

   a. _____

   b. _____

   c. _____

   Isaiah 53:6 (Children as Sinners)

   a. _____

   b. _____

   c. _____

EXERCISE 4

A. The story of Joseph and his brothers is a well-known biblical example of parent-child and sibling relationships. Read the account in Genesis 37:2–28. In this classic case of sibling rivalry and resentment we see several causes for the conflict between Joseph and his brothers. List at least three sources of the brothers' resentment.*

   1. _____

   2. _____

   3. _____

B. If you have more than one child in your home, your family probably has to deal with a good amount of sibling jealousy and rivalry. Discuss these sibling conflicts and write down at least three causes of them.

1. _____

2. _____

3. _____

EXERCISE 5

Here are a few of the many Scripture verses that give us guidelines on relating positively to others. Read these verses and list five qualities, attitudes, or actions that characterize positive personal relationships.*

> It is hard to stop a quarrel once it starts, so don't let it begin. (Prov. 17:14 LB)
>
> So comfort and encourage each other . . . (1 Thess. 4:18 LB)
>
> Admit your faults to one another and pray for each other so that you may be healed. The earnest prayer of a righteous man has great power and wonderful results. (James 5:16 LB)

1. _____

2. _____

3. _____

4. _____

5. _____

Which of these are strengths in your relationships with your children?

1. _____

2. _____

3. _____

Which are weaknesses?

1. _____

2. _____

3. _____

Answer Keys

Exercise 2(A)

1. He provides for our needs (v. 1).
2. He helps us rest, and He refreshes us (v. 2).
3. He guides us (v. 3).
4. He encourages and comforts us in difficult times (v. 4).
5. He protects us in the presence of enemies (v. 5).

Exercise 2(B)

1. He protects us and helps us (Ps. 18:19; Ps. 59:10; Prov. 2:8).
2. He enjoys us (Ps. 18:19).
3. He loves us eternally and unconditionally (Jer. 31:3; Rom. 8:38–39).
4. He keeps us (Rom. 8:38–39).
5. His love is consistent (Ps. 59:10).
6. He is patient, compassionate, and gentle (Ps. 86:15; Ps. 145:8–9).

Exercise 3

1. (a) We are created in God's image and, therefore, are very important to Him.
   (b) We are also sinful.
2. Psalm 8:4–9
   (a) They have a right to be treated with dignity and respect.
   (b) They have great potential.
   (c) They are significant to God.
   (d) They will be happiest when they live as their Creator designed them to live.
3. Isaiah 53:6
   (a) All children will sin and rebel.
   (b) They will need guidance and correction.
   (c) Permissive parenting will not work.
   (d) Children are in need of God's grace.

Exercise 4

1. Joseph was a tattletale (v. 2).
2. The father, Jacob, favored Joseph over his other sons (vv. 3–4).
3. Joseph had an air of superiority (vv. 5–8).

Exercise 5

1. Comfort (1 Thess. 4:18)
2. Encouragement (1 Thess. 4:18)
3. Openness—admitting our mistakes (James 5:16)
4. Praying for one another (James 5:16)
5. Avoiding quarrels (Prov. 17:14)

– 3 –

PURPOSES OF PARENTING

The first institution established by God was the family. The Bible repeatedly emphasizes its importance. As parents, however, we often become so involved in the "nitty-gritty" of family life that we lose sight of Scripture's broad perspective on the family. We are so busy settling family squabbles, motivating children to do their chores, and running from one activity to another that we seldom pause to ask ourselves, "Just why did God give children parents?"

As parents we can take one of two perspectives on the family. Like most non-Christian parents we can get caught up in the passing joys, ceaseless activities, and ever-present frustrations of parenthood, and we can find a goodly measure of fulfillment in living from this perspective. But if we pause to consider God's great design in the universe and our potential in sharing in that purpose with Him, we can lift our parenting to an entirely different level. This viewpoint doesn't wipe out the daily hassles that every parent faces, but it does put them in an entirely different perspective.

169

Once we realize God's great plan to people the earth with His children and to establish His righteous kingdom in the future, we can look beyond our daily responsibilities and frustrations. We can see ourselves as God's agents for influencing society through our children. And we can see the job of parenting as a spiritual activity—one that God established and one that He will help us carry out.

EXERCISE 1

In chapter 3, six purposes of parenting are presented. Two of those purposes—bringing joy to parents and glorifying God—are the focus of this chapter.

Discuss with your spouse some of the ways you would like to see God glorified through your family. Write your thoughts below.

1. _____

_____

_____

2. _____

_____

_____

3. _____

_____

_____

4. _____

_____

_____

5. _____

_____

_____

EXERCISE 2 (For the Wife)

Select the two most joyous times you have experienced with each of your children, or the two major contributions each of your children has made to your life. Share these joys with your husband (or study group) and jot them down below. Identify the special time or contribution and also describe your feeling of joy, fulfillment, or reward. Within one week after completing this exercise take time to sit down with each one of your children and share with them how much they mean to you and relate specific instances in which they have brought joy into your life. This makes children feel very special and gives them a deep sense of belonging and of importance. (Use separate sheets for each of your children.)

Child

   1. Contribution or joyous occasion

   _____

   _____

   _____

   Your feeling about the time or contribution

   _____

   _____

   _____

   2. Contribution or joyous occasion

   _____

   _____

   _____

   Your feeling about the time or contribution

   _____

   _____

172 Parenting With Love and Limits

EXERCISE 2 (For the Husband)

Select the two most joyous times you have experienced
with each of your children, or the two major contributions
each of your children has made to your life. Share these
joys with your wife (or study group) and jot them down
below. Identify the special time or contribution and also
describe your feeling of joy, fulfillment, or reward. Within
one week after completing this exercise take time to sit
down with each one of your children and share with them
how much they mean to you and relate specific instances
in which they have brought joy into your life. This makes
children feel very special and gives them a deep sense of
belonging and of importance. (Use separate sheets for each
of your children.)

Child

   1. Contribution or joyous occasion

_____

_____

_____

_____

   Your feeling about the time or contribution

_____

_____

_____

   2. Contribution or joyous occasion

_____

_____

_____

_____

Your feeling about the time or contribution

_____

_____

_____

EXERCISE 3

Sometimes we become so busy and so caught up in our daily activities that we stop having fun as families. This is a sure sign that our priorities are mixed up. This is the time to take action: Sit down with the entire family and plan something that is really fun for every family member to be involved in. If one activity won't satisfy everyone, plan two! Schedule this fun time so that it occurs within the next three weeks.

After you have enjoyed that time together, arrange to do something special as a family at least once a month for the next three months. After that you may want to continue this practice Some families set aside one evening each week for "family night." Mother or dad fixes a special meal (including the children's favorite dishes); and after everyone helps clean up the kitchen, there is an hour or two of games or other family fun. (Note to husbands: Family night is not to take the place of your own special time with your wife!) List below several activities your family can enjoy together.

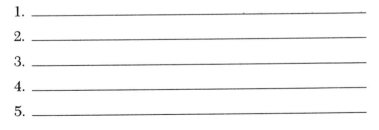

1. _____

2. _____

3. _____

4. _____

5. _____

— 4 —

FAMILY LEADERSHIP

Every parent has a style of relating to her or his own children. Some of us are somewhat distant. Others are more intimately involved. Some of us rule our families sternly. Others are more "loose." Some make much use of punishment and pressure. Others seldom use these means. Undergirding each of these approaches, however, is the more basic issue of our approach to authority in the family. We see in chapter 4 that styles of family leadership vary along a continuum that extends from "authoritarian" to "permissive." At one end we have an emphasis on strict obedience, parental rights, power, punishment, and pressure. On the other end we have an emphasis on children's rights, the de-emphasis of power, and the need for children to practice self-determination. Between these two extremes lies the biblical model of family leadership or family government—loving or benevolent authority.

The chart on the following page summarizes the essential aspects of these three approaches. Of course, we would not hold to *every* one of the entries listed under our style of government. We all fall at slightly different places on the continuum. Most authoritarian parents, for example, certainly have some concern for their child's inner attitudes. They will not *always* overuse authority. They will also at times try to win cooperation through love and stimulation. And their children won't be totally dependent or rebellious. Similarly, permissive parents will occasionally lose their tempers and resort to force pressure, and coercion. These categories are merely used to reflect general styles of leadership and family government. The so-called democratic form of parenting is very similar to the permissive style in its basic elements, except for a strong emphasis on shared solutions and mutual responsibilities. It does also tend to promote much more positive inner attitudes than does the permissive approach. However, it fails to deal with the presence of sin and the child's need for a good measure of outside direction and guidance. For these reasons we include it under the general category of permissiveness.

Both permissive and authoritarian styles of parenting have serious limitations. The drawbacks of authoritarianism include:

- Since conformity and obedience are obtained by force, authoritarianism requires the presence of the authority to keep the child "in line."

- Since motivation is largely by fear and external pressure, authoritarianism works against the development of an inner (biblical) set of love-motivated controls.

- Due to the excessive use of pressure and power and the strong focus on external conformity and obedience, authoritarianism breeds one or more of the following: personality rigidity, overdependency, or rebellion.

- Due to the parental pressure and the lack of sensitivity to the child's inner needs and feelings, authoritarianism undermines the child's sense of significance and value and attacks self-esteem. It can also breed excessive guilt and anger.

The problems of permissive (and democratic) parenting include:

- The denial or minimizing of the sinfulness of children

- The development of hurtful life patterns that are the result of inadequate parental guidance

- The difficulty in relating to authority of any kind experienced by children reared without limits and loving controls

- The adverse effects of a lack of limits on a child's self-esteem

The biblical model of family leadership style is characterized by:

- Deep respect for children as bearers of the image of God

- Sensitivity to both the needs and capabilities of children

- Parental commitment to provide for their children's needs

- Delegated parental authority carried out as a trust from God

- Keen awareness of the parents' own sinfulness, fallibility, and need of grace

- Lovingly established limits and restrictions

- Discipline, training, and correction based on biblical guidelines and instructions

- A warm and loving family atmosphere

Chart A
STYLES OF FAMILY LEADERSHIP

	Authoritarian	Permissive	Loving Authority
Primary Focus	External conformity or obedience	Attitudes	Attitudes that result in proper behavior
Use of Parental Authority and Power	Unquestioning use	Not used	Carried out as a delegated responsibility from the Lord
Motivation	Fear, pressure, power, and coercion	Love, stimulation, and cooperation	Love, stimulation, cooperation, and appropriate correction or use of consequences
View of Human Nature	Basically sinful	Basically good	Image-bearers, yet sinful
Attitude Toward Child	Children to be seen and not heard	Children to be trusted implicitly and respected	Children to be deeply respected as creations of God but also recognized as being sinful and having rebellious tendencies
Resulting Behavior	Blind conformity or rebellion	Insufficient controls or search for limits	Balance of cooperativeness, conformity, and creative assertiveness
Resulting Emotions	Fear, guilt, or resentment	A level of self-respect because of parental trust, but anxiety or insecurity because of lack of limits	Self-respect accompanied by security and love

EXERCISE 1 (Abuses of Authority)

A. Here is a quotation from an author who advocates an authoritarian approach to rearing children. After reading the quotation complete the exercise below.

> Son, this has gone beyond the matter of your hair now. Your mother and I are concerned about your rebellion against our will. That's the one thing God hates most in a child. We've decided we dare not feed a rebel in our home. We cannot use the daily bread which God provides to feed someone who defies His will. As long as you persist in the rebellion, you will not eat in this home. Your mother is not to fix another meal for you until you get your hair cut as we have asked and apologize for your rebellion.[1]

1. What features of this approach reveal its authoritarian nature? (see chart A)

_____

_____

_____

_____

2. If you were a teen-ager and your parents treated you this way, how would you have felt toward them?

_____

_____

_____

What would you have done?

_____

_____

_____

[1]C. S. Lovett, *What's a Parent to Do?* (Baldwin Park, Calif.: Personal Christianity, 1971), p. 133.

3. What do you think had been happening for years in this family to allow such a confrontation to develop?

_____

_____

_____

_____

B. Here is another example of authoritarianism. Read it and complete the questions below.

One of our three children was basically a very obedient child. We often had to punish her severely for a minor problem. We knew all the clichés about how punishment had to fit the crime, but we could not apply those clichés. God led us to discipline on the little things so she'd learn to repent and thus receive blessings from God.[2]

1. How did you react to the above statement, especially about being punished severely for a minor problem? Do you agree or disagree? Discuss your reaction with your spouse or study group and then insert it below. If you and your spouse reacted differently, write both reactions.

_____

_____

_____

_____

_____

_____

_____

[2]Wendell Robley and Grace Robley, *Spank Me If You Love Me* (Harrison, Ark.: New Leaf Press, 1976), pp. 15–16.

2. If you were basically a very obedient child but were punished severely for minor problems, how would you feel?

_____

_____

_____

3. What do you think a girl raised under this system would be like when she grew up?

_____

_____

_____

EXERCISE 2 (Permissiveness)

Here is a quotation from Thomas Gordon, the founder of Parent Effectiveness Training. This program, while offering some excellent insights on communication, strays far from biblical teaching in several areas.

1. After reading the quotation, refer to chart A on page 177 to determine which aspects of family leadership best describe this approach.

A much sounder principle than "children want their parents to use their authority and set limits" is the following: Children want and need information from their parents that will tell them the parents' feeling about their behavior so that they themselves can modify behavior that might be unacceptable to the parents. However, children do not want the parents to try to limit or modify their behavior by using or threatening to use their authority. In short, children want to limit their behavior *themselves* if it becomes apparent to them that their behavior must be limited or modified. Children, like adults, prefer to be their own authority over their behavior.[3]

[3] Thomas Gordon, *Parent Effectiveness Training* (New York: New American Library, Plume Books, 1975), pp. 187–88.

2. Do you agree that "children, like adults, prefer to be their own authority"? Why or why not?

_____

_____

_____

3. According to the Bible, is any person to be her or his own authority? _____

Why or why not? _____

_____

_____

_____

Give Scripture that supports your answer.

_____

_____

_____

4. What positive principles or attitudes does this quotation reflect that are consistent with Scripture when balanced with the need for authority?

_____

_____

_____

EXERCISE 3

Our attitudes and approaches to child rearing are usually shaped by the type of training we received as children. We tend to adopt either the same attitudes as our parents had or the opposite attitudes. In the following exercises on child rearing approaches, husbands and wives should use different color pens to complete the chart.

FATHER'S APPROACH

Primary Focus	External conformity or obedience	Attitudes	Attitudes that result in proper behavior
Parental Authority and Power	Unquestioning use	Not used	Carried out as a responsibility given by God
Motivation	Fear, pressure, power, and coercion	Love, stimulation, and cooperation	Love, stimulation, cooperation, and appropriate correction
View of Human Nature	Basically sinful	Basically good	Image-bearers, yet sinful
Attitude Toward Child	Children to be seen and not heard	Children to be trusted implicitly and respected	Children to be deeply respected as creations of God but also recognized as being sinful

A. In the chart above circle the entry for each aspect of parenting that best characterizes each of your fathers's approaches to child rearing.

B. In the following chart circle the entry for each aspect of parenting that best characterizes each of your mothers's approaches to child rearing.

C. The following questions are designed to help you see how your parents influenced your attitudes toward child rearing.

MOTHER'S APPROACH

Primary Focus	External conformity or obedience	Attitudes	Attitudes that result in proper behavior
Parental Authority and Power	Unquestioning use	Not used	Carried out as a responsibility given by God
Motivation	Fear, pressure, power, and coercion	Love, stimulation, and cooperation	Love, stimulation, cooperation, and appropriate correction
View of Human Nature	Basically sinful	Basically good	Image-bearers, yet sinful
Attitude Toward Child	Children to be seen and not heard	Children to be trusted implicitly and respected	Children to be deeply respected as creations of God but also recognized as being sinful

1. In what ways is your attitude toward child rearing similar to your father's?

_____

_____

_____

Why, do you think, are you similar to your father in these ways?

_____

_____

_____

2. In what ways is your attitude different from your father's?

_____

_____

_____

Why do you think it is different?

_____

_____

_____

3. In what way is your attitude toward child rearing similar to your mother's?

_____

_____

_____

Why, do you think, are you similar to your mother in these ways?

_____

_____

_____

4. In what ways is your attitude toward child rearing different from your mother's?

_____

_____

_____

Why do you think it is different?

_____

_____

_____

EXERCISE 4 (For the Wife)

Now it's time to rate yourself on the major aspects of parenting.

A. In the chart on the next page, circle the statement for each aspect of parenting that best characterizes your approach to child rearing.

B. Ask your spouse (or a good friend) to use the same chart, and with a different color pen circle the statement for each aspect of parenting that he or she believes best characterizes your approach to child rearing.

EXERCISE 4 (For the Husband)

Now it's time to rate yourself on the major aspects of parenting.

A. In the chart following your wife's, circle the statement for each aspect of parenting that best characterizes your approach to child rearing.

B. Ask your spouse (or a good friend) to use the same chart, and with a different color pen circle the statement for each aspect of parenting that he or she believes best characterizes your approach to child rearing.

WIFE'S APPROACH

Primary Focus	"I focus largely on my children's actions and obedience."	"I focus largely on my children's feelings and their inner attitudes."	"I focus on both my children's inner feelings and their behavior."
Use of Parental Authority and Power	"I believe parents should be the unquestioned authority."	"I believe children should be allowed to make all of their own decisions."	"I believe children need some parental authority, but they should also be learning to participate in decision making."
Motivation	"I frequently rely on fear, pressure, power, and coercion to motivate my children."	"I rely almost exclusively on love, stimulation, and cooperation to motivate my children."	"I rely largely on love, stimulation, and cooperation in conjunction with loving correction and the use of consequences to motivate my children."
View of Human Nature	"I believe people are basically sinful."	"I believe people are basically good."	"I believe people are image-bearers, but they are also sinful."
Attitude Toward Child	"Children should be seen and not heard."	"Children should be implicitly trusted and respected, and they should be allowed to make all of their own choices."	"Children should be respected and made to feel important, but they should also be sensitive to their sinful tendencies."

HUSBAND'S APPROACH

Primary Focus	"I focus largely on my children's actions and obedience."	"I focus largely on my children's feelings and their inner attitudes."	"I focus on both my children's inner feelings and their behavior."
Use of Parental Authority and Power	"I believe parents should be the unquestioned authority."	"I believe children should be allowed to make all of their own decisions."	"I believe children need some parental authority, but they should also be learning to participate in decision making."
Motivation	"I frequently rely on fear, pressure, power, and coercion to motivate my children."	"I rely almost exclusively on love, stimulation, and cooperation to motivate my children."	"I rely largely on love, stimulation, and cooperation in conjunction with loving correction and the use of consequences to motivate my children."
View of Human Nature	"I believe people are basically sinful."	"I believe people are basically good."	"I believe people are image-bearers, but they are also sinful."
Attitude Toward Child	"Children should be seen and not heard."	"Children should be implicitly trusted and respected, and they should be allowed to make all of their own choices."	"Children should be respected and made to feel important, but they should also be sensitive to their sinful tendencies."

-5-

ꟼARENTS
AS
ꟼROVIDERS

As parents we have the responsibility to provide for our children's physical, spiritual, and emotional needs. In chapter 5 God's provision for His children is presented as the model for our provision for our children. The present chapter is designed to show how we can translate those insights about God's care for us into effective parenting.

EXERCISE 1

A. All children have basic needs. Make a list of some of the most important of these needs, using the categories below.

Physical Needs

_____

_____

_____

_____

_____

_____

Spiritual Needs

_____

_____

_____

_____

_____

Emotional Needs

_____

_____

_____

_____

Social and Intellectual Needs

_____

_____

_____

_____

B. In each category, indicate which of your children's needs are easiest for you to meet.

Physical Needs

_____

_____

Spiritual Needs

_____

_____

Emotional Needs

_____

_____

Social and Intellectual Needs

_____

_____

C. In each category, indicate which of your children's needs you have the most difficulty meeting.

Physical Needs

_____

_____

Spiritual Needs

_____

_____

Emotional Needs

_____

_____

Social and Intellectual Needs

_____

_____

D. In this section, you and your spouse will be discussing your children. For each child select one important need that is not being met. Then decide on some specific things you are going to do to help meet each of these needs. For example, if one of your children has few friends in the neighborhood you might encourage her or him to invite a friend home after school. If one of your children is fearful and lacking in confidence, you can begin to eliminate your criticism, learn to praise the child, and begin working (or playing) together on a project. And if one of your children lacks an assurance of your love because you are too busy to spend good times together or because you have difficulty listening attentively to feelings, ideas, and experiences, find ways to attack these problems.

Child

1. Need _____

2. Plan of Action _____

_____

_____

_____

EXERCISE 2

It is difficult to reach out and meet others' needs when our own have not been met. If we are too busy, too easily frustrated, too pressured, too anxious, or if we lack a sense of belonging, it is doubly hard to help our children with these problems! In fact, our children often bring some of our own deepest needs and biggest hurts to the surface.

1. List two or three of your own needs that, if met, would make it easier for you to be an effective parent.

_____

_____

_____

_____

2. Spend some time discussing these needs with your spouse, your study group, or a friend. Tell them how you feel about these needs or problems. Then discuss a plan of action. How can you better meet

these needs? Can the person or the group in whom you are confiding help you? Can you rearrange your schedule? Can you spend more time with your spouse? Can you work on communication or other aspects of your relationship with your spouse? Can you find a person to help bear your burden? Write your plan below.

_____

_____

_____

_____

_____

_____

3. Sometimes our own unmet emotional needs are part of the reason we err on the side of either authoritarian or permissive parenting. If we lack self-confidence, for example, we might throw up our hands and let our children get by with murder. Or we might go to the opposite extreme and try to cover up our anxiety by being rigid, controlling, and authoritarian. Do you see any relationship between your rating of your parenting in chapter 4 and the emotional needs you listed above? Discuss this with your spouse or with the study group.

_____

_____

_____

_____

– 6 –

PARENTS
AS
TRAINERS

As parents we have a threefold responsibility to our children:

- provide for their needs

- train, guide, and instruct them

- correct them

The second of these responsibilities, training, is the focus of this chapter.

Training encompasses all of our positive guidance and instruction. In some ways this is the most rewarding and at the same time one of the most frequently overlooked aspects of rearing children. It is our opportunity to invest in our children's lives when there is no particular problem that limits our options. It is our opportunity to instill in our children positive attitudes about themselves and lasting moral values. Training can be one of the most satisfying aspects of being a parent.

EXERCISE 1

A. In the Bible there is a difference between discipline and punishment. Fill in the chart below as a refresher on these differences.

FOR HUSBAND AND WIFE

	Punishment	Discipline
Purpose		
Focus		
Attitude		

B. Discuss with your spouse or study group each of the following statements by parents. Decide whether they are punishment (or threats of punishment) or discipline and why.

1. "I'm sick and tired of telling you to take out the trash, John! Get that stuff out of here, or you'll have no supper!"

This statement is an example of _____.

Why? _____

_____

_____

2. "I'll teach you never to do that again if it's the last thing I ever do!"

This statement is an example of ＿＿＿＿＿＿.

Why? ＿＿＿＿＿＿＿＿＿＿＿＿＿＿＿＿

＿＿＿＿＿＿＿＿＿＿＿＿＿＿＿＿＿＿＿＿

＿＿＿＿＿＿＿＿＿＿＿＿＿＿＿＿＿＿＿＿

3. "I'm sorry, Ben, but I told you you could not watch television until the yard work was finished."

This statement is an example of ＿＿＿＿＿＿.

Why? ＿＿＿＿＿＿＿＿＿＿＿＿＿＿＿＿

＿＿＿＿＿＿＿＿＿＿＿＿＿＿＿＿＿＿＿＿

＿＿＿＿＿＿＿＿＿＿＿＿＿＿＿＿＿＿＿＿

4. "We're going to have to find a way to get that homework done, honey. Let's sit down and talk it over."

This statement is an example of ＿＿＿＿＿＿.

Why? ＿＿＿＿＿＿＿＿＿＿＿＿＿＿＿＿

＿＿＿＿＿＿＿＿＿＿＿＿＿＿＿＿＿＿＿＿

＿＿＿＿＿＿＿＿＿＿＿＿＿＿＿＿＿＿＿＿

5. "I've had it with you kids! You go to your room!"

This statement is an example of ＿＿＿＿＿＿.

Why? ＿＿＿＿＿＿＿＿＿＿＿＿＿＿＿＿

＿＿＿＿＿＿＿＿＿＿＿＿＿＿＿＿＿＿＿＿

＿＿＿＿＿＿＿＿＿＿＿＿＿＿＿＿＿＿＿＿

6. "If you children can't get along you will each have to spend twenty minutes in your room so you can learn to play together better."

This statement is an example of _____.
Why? _____

_____

_____

C. Discuss with your spouse or study group a recent time
you attempted to correct one of your children. Decide
together whether you were punishing them or accepting them.

EXERCISE 2

Review the section entitled "Training" in chapter 6 and
complete the following quiz. Check your answer key at the
end of this section and reread the portions of chapter 6 that
discuss any items you missed.

1. The Hebrew word translated "train" (*khanakh*) in
   Proverbs 22:6 means to correct children after they
   have misbehaved.
   True or False? _____

2. The phrase "the way" in Proverbs 22:6 means that

   _____

   _____

3. The Greek word translated "discipline" (*paideia*)
   refers to both preventive training and correction.
   True or False? _____

4. According to Deuteronomy 6:1–9, religious teaching is not to be done in a vacuum. What three things
   does this passage instruct parents to do in conjunc-
   tion with instruction of their children?

   a. _____

   b. _____

   c. _____

5. According to Deuteronomy 6:1–9, when and where should spiritual instruction be carried out?

_____

_____

_____

EXERCISE 3

The Bible suggests that spiritual instruction and training is a total way of life. It cannot be effective if removed from the nitty-gritty realities of daily life. Discuss with your spouse or study group several specific life situations in which you have had an opportunity to spontaneously share spiritual truths or principles with your children. List below other opportunities you might utilize.

1. Situation _____

_____

_____

Lesson or concept _____

_____

_____

2. Situation _____

_____

_____

Lesson or concept _____

_____

_____

Answer Key

Exercise 2

1. False
2. Parents are to train their children so that they will develop fully and become the unique beings that God has destined them to be.
3. True
4. (a) Live (do) God's commandments themselves
   (b) Love God
   (c) Learn God's Words themselves
5. (a) In the home
   (b) Along the way (in the general course of life)
   (c) When they lay down
   (d) When they rose up (at all times)

- 7 -

PARENTS
AS
CORRECTORS

Chapter 7 focuses on our parental role as correctors. It suggested that correction should always follow proper instruction and provision, but that it would have its place. According to Scripture correction includes instruction, communication, experience, natural consequences, and physical pain. No one technique of correction is adequate. There are times when children must learn by suffering the consequences of their misbehavior, and there are times they will learn by counsel and communication. There are times they will learn by another's example, and there are times they will need to be corrected by a spanking.

EXERCISE 1

The story of the lost son in Luke 15 is a good example of a parent allowing a child to profit from the consequences of her or his own behavior. Reread that story and complete the questions below.

    1. What would you have wanted to say or do to your young-adult son if he had asked you for his share of your estate?

_____

_____

_____

2. Do you think you would have given him the money and let him go?

_____

3. What would you have wanted to say when you saw your son returning?

_____

_____

4. If you were the son (or daughter) in this story, how would you have felt if your father had not let you go?

_____

_____

5. How would you have felt if your father did let you go?

_____

_____

6. When you finally came to your senses, how do you think you would have felt?

_____

_____

7. If your father took you back and held a banquet for you, how would you have felt?

_____

_____

8. If you were the son (or daughter), what would have been the lasting result of this experience in your life?

_____

_____

_____

EXERCISE 2 (For the Wife)

Chapter 7 lists nine biblically based principles for correcting children.

A. Rate yourself on each of these nine statements by marking one of the four boxes in the chart.

B. Ask your spouse, your child, or a friend to rate you on the same nine statements. The person should use a different color pen than your own.

C. Comment on any discrepancies between your self-rating and the rating others gave you.

_____

_____

_____

_____

_____

EXERCISE 2 (For the Husband)

Chapter 7 lists nine biblically based principles for correcting children.

A. Rate yourself on each of these nine statements by marking one of the four boxes in the chart.

B. Ask your spouse, your child, or a friend to rate you on the same nine statements. The person should use a different color pen than your own.

FOR WIFE

	Almost Always	Usually	Some-times	Rarely
"My correction is preceded by my own good example."				
"I provide for my children's physical, social, emotional, and spiritual needs."				
"I instruct my children carefully before I correct them."				
"I calmly correct my children in love rather than out of frustration."				
"I correct my children for their welfare."				
"I punish my children and stir up fear and resentment."				
"I prayerfully plan my correction ahead of time."				
"My correction is sensitive."				
"My correction promotes increased understanding."				

C. Comment on any discrepancies between your self-rating and the rating others gave you.

_____

_____

_____

FOR HUSBAND

	Almost Always	Usually	Some-times	Rarely
"My correction is preceded by my own good example."				
"I provide for my children's physical, social, emotional, and spiritual needs."				
"I instruct my children carefully before I correct them."				
"I calmly correct my children in love rather than out of frustration."				
"I correct my children for their welfare."				
"I punish my children and stir up fear and resentment."				
"I prayerfully plan my correction ahead of time."				
"My correction is sensitive."				
"My correction promotes increased understanding."				

EXERCISE 3

If you are in a class or study group, have people role-play the way they would handle a typical disciplinary situation. First have someone correct in the wrong way (anger, blaming, impulsiveness, etc.). As this person acts this out, think how you would feel if you were the child and describe it briefly.

_____

_____

_____

_____

Then have someone role-play a positive corrective response. How would you feel now?

_____

_____

_____

_____

_____

–8–

DISCIPLINE
BY
GRACE

The Bible describes two ways of relating to God. The first is on the basis of performance, works, and effort—a method known as "law"—and the second is on the basis of acceptance, appreciation, and forgiveness—a method known as "grace." Under law, we are obliged to perform. When we do not live up to the standard, we are subject to punishment (as contrasted to discipline) and rejection. Under grace, we perform in response to God's love and forgiveness. We work *from* our acceptance rather than *for* it.

These same two methods of relating apply to the parent-child relationship. As parents we can force children to work *for* our love and to avoid rejection and punishment. Here we focus on external behavior. When we do this we give the message, "Work and you will be accepted." On the other hand, we can love our children unconditionally and focus primarily on their inner needs. We can motivate by love and avoid the use of pressure. When we respond this way we give the message, "We love you just the way you are. You are extremely important to us, and we want to help you grow to your full potential."

Nearly everything we have covered in our study so far can be included under this view of law and grace. Authoritarianism is a classic example of law. Parent provision and loving discipline are reflections of God's grace.

EXERCISE 1

Chapter 8 discusses five contrasts between law and grace. Write out these five contrasting principles below.

1. (Law) _____

   _____

   (Grace) _____

   _____

2. (Law) _____

   _____

   (Grace) _____

   _____

3. (Law) _____

   _____

   (Grace) _____

   _____

4. (Law) _____

   _____

   (Grace) _____

   _____

5. (Law) _____

   _____

   (Grace) _____

   _____

EXERCISE 2 (For the Wife)

A. The following chart is designed to help you see whether you are relating to your children on the basis of principles of law or principles of grace. For each of the statements in the chart place a mark in the box that best describes your style of relating to your children.

B. Now ask your husband or a good friend to rate you, using a different color pen than your own. Or if your children are at least eight years old, you might ask them to rate you and then sit down together with them to discuss their evaluation. This can be an excellent opportunity for you and your child to communicate about an area that is seldom touched on in many families.

C. Discuss the evaluations with your spouse or study group. Share one area you believe is a strength and one that is more difficult for you. Select one aspect you would like to change and write it below. Ask your spouse or others in your study group to pray regularly with you concerning this need and continue sharing your progress with them. They may also be of help by sharing similar struggles and by helping you see why you tend to react the way you do.

_____

_____

_____

_____

_____

_____

_____

FOR WIFE

	Almost Always	Usually	Some-times	Rarely
"My children know I accept them just the way they are."				
"My children believe I want to give them good things just because they are my children."				
"I correct (rather than punish) my children after they misbehave."				
"I focus on my children's emotions and attitudes rather than on their performance and actions."				
"I rely on love (rather than pressure and fear) to motivate my children."				

EXERCISE 2 (For the Husband)

A. The following chart is designed to help you see whether you are relating to your children on the basis of principles of law or principles of grace. For each of the statements in the chart place a mark in the box that best describes your style of relating to your children.

B. Now ask your wife or a good friend to rate you, using a different color pen than your own. Or if your children are at least eight years old, you might ask them to rate you and then sit down together with them to discuss their evaluation. This can be an excellent opportunity for you and your child to communicate about an area that is seldom touched on in many families.

FOR HUSBAND

	Almost Always	Usually	Some-times	Rarely
"My children know I accept them just the way they are."				
"My children believe I want to give them good things just because they are my children."				
"I correct (rather than punish) my children after they misbehave."				
"I focus on my children's emotions and attitudes rather than on their performance and actions."				
"I rely on love (rather than pressure and fear) to motivate my children."				

C. Discuss the evaluations above with your spouse or study group. Share one area you believe is a strength and one that is more difficult for you. Select one aspect you would like to change and write it below. Ask your spouse or others in your study group to pray regularly with you concerning this need and continue sharing your progress with them. They may also be of help by sharing similar struggles and by helping you see why you tend to react the way you do.

_____

_____

_____

_____

EXERCISE 3

Fear and guilt are two of the major ways of attempting to motivate under law. As God's children we are never motivated by these negative emotions. 1 John 4:17–18 tells us:

> Love is made complete among us so that we will have confidence on the day of judgment, because in this world we are like him. There is no fear in love. But perfect love drives out fear, because fear has to do with punishment. The man who fears is not made perfect in love.

Romans 8:1 says:

> Therefore, there is now no condemnation for those who are in Christ Jesus.

A. If you are in a class or study group, have one member role-play a parent attempting to motivate a child to do the chores (trash, dishes, room cleaning, etc.) by using fear and guilt. How would you feel if your parents tried to motivate you in this way?

_____

_____

_____

B. Now role-play without fear and guilt but with loving firmness. How would you feel if your parents motivated you in this way?

_____

_____

_____

C. If you are not in a study group, write out first a legalistic and then a "grace-ful" way of motivating your child to do the chores.

Legalistic (fear and guilt)

_____

_____

_____

_____

_____

_____

Grace-ful (firmly but lovingly and by using a consequence)

_____

_____

_____

_____

_____

_____

- 9 -

A CHILD'S VIEW OF GOD

In the intimate parent-child relationship we gain our first glimpse of what God is like. This is one reason God created the family. To the degree that parents are loving, sensitive, and dependable, children find it easy to see God in a similar way. But when earthly parents are impatient, easily frustrated, worrisome, or unforgiving, it is difficult for children to develop an accurate understanding of the character of God.

EXERCISE 1

Based on our own life experiences most of us find it easier to relate to some of God's attributes than to others.

1. Of the nine attributes of God listed below, circle the ones you find easiest to understand and to relate to.

Sensitive	Trustable
Fair	Consistent
Patient	Righteous
Encouraging	Loving
Forgiving	

2. Which attributes of God listed above do you sometimes have greater difficulty understanding or accepting?

_____

_____

3. If it is easier for you to relate to some of God's attributes than to others, why, do you think, is this so?

_____

_____

_____

4. If it is as easy (or difficult) for you to accept or believe in one of God's attributes as it is to accept or believe in another, why, do you think, is this so?

_____

_____

_____

EXERCISE 2

A. Based on your children's relationship with you, what image of God do you think they are developing? In the lists below circle a rating for each category, based on the following key: (1) excellent; (2) pretty good; (3) fair; and (4) poor. (Use separate sheets as necessary.)

Child

Sensitive and gentle	1 2 3 4	Insensitive
Fair	1 2 3 4	Biased or unjust
Patient	1 2 3 4	Impatient
Encouraging	1 2 3 4	Critical and/or discouraging
Forgiving	1 2 3 4	Harbors a grudge

Trustable	1	2	3	4	Unreliable
Consistent	1	2	3	4	Inconsistent
Righteous	1	2	3	4	Unrighteous or evil
Loving	1	2	3	4	Selfish and/or angry

B. If your children are school age, sit down with one or more of them and ask them to rate you on these items. Simply ask them what they think you are like on each point; do not ask them to relate this to their image of God. After they have rated you, take this opportunity to discuss your relationship with them. Which of these areas would they like to see you working on? How do they feel when you do well or poorly in some area? How would they like to see you change? Then thank them for their input and let them know you will be working on their suggestions. Remind them you won't be perfect and that it may take a while to grow, but assure them that you value their opinions and really want to learn from their suggestions. This is an excellent way to find out how your children really feel about your family life. (Use separate sheets as necessary.)

Child's Rating of You

Sensitive and gentle	1	2	3	4	Insensitive
Fair	1	2	3	4	Biased or unjust
Patient	1	2	3	4	Impatient
Encouraging	1	2	3	4	Critical and/or discouraging
Forgiving	1	2	3	4	Harbors a grudge
Trustable	1	2	3	4	Unreliable
Consistent	1	2	3	4	Inconsistent
Righteous	1	2	3	4	Unrighteous or evil
Loving	1	2	3	4	Selfish and/or angry

EXERCISE 3

Choose one aspect of your relationship with your children that you would like to improve in order to help them develop a better understanding of God's character. Write out how you might improve below, discuss it with your spouse, and give special attention to that aspect of your relationship with your child for the next week.

_____

_____

_____

_____

SELF-ESTEEM
IN
CHILDREN

According to the Bible we should have a balanced attitude toward ourselves. We should first of all realize that we are highly significant. We are people of worth and value. Then we should see ourselves as deeply fallen. We have sinned and rebelled against God. Finally, we should see ourselves as greatly loved and restored. In spite of our sinfulness, God reached out to save us. He loves us and sees us as valuable.

Self-esteem is one of your child's most valuable possessions. Children with a basically positive attitude toward themselves are more successful academically, better liked, and in general more happy and fulfilled than those with a more negative self-image. This chapter is designed to help cement in our minds the biblical basis for self-esteem.

EXERCISE 1

Chapter 10 discusses six biblical foundations for seeing ourselves and our children as highly significant. List those reasons and write out as least one relevant Scripture verse.

1. Foundation: _____

   Scripture: _____

2. Foundation: _____

   Scripture: _____

3. Foundation: _____

   Scripture: _____

4. Foundation: _____

   Scripture: _____

5. Foundation: _____

   Scripture: _____

6. Foundation: _____

   Scripture: _____

EXERCISE 2

Our self-concept involves feelings of security, worth, confidence, and belonging. For each of your children, check the box that you think best describes the child's attitude toward herself or himself in these four areas. Then discuss these with your spouse and list three or four reasons for your child's rating in each area. (Use separate sheets as necessary.)

CHILD

	Almost Always	Usually	Some-times	Rarely
Feels a strong sense of security				
Feels a strong sense of worth				
Feels a strong sense of confidence				
Feels a strong sense of belonging				

Reasons for your child's level of security:

_____

_____

_____

Reasons for your child's level of worth:

_____

_____

_____

Reasons for your child's level of confidence:

_____

_____

_____

Reasons for your child's level of belonging:

_____

_____

_____

EXERCISE 3

A. List the eleven ways of building up another person's self-esteem given in chapter ten.

1. _____

   _____

2. _____

   _____

3. _____

   _____

4. _____

   _____

5. _____

   _____

6. _____

   _____

7. _____

   _____

8. _____

_____

9. _____

_____

10. _____

_____

11. _____

_____

B. Select one of the above guides that you need to work on with your children. Discuss it with your spouse or study group and make a concentrated effort to put it into practice every day for one week. Then share with your spouse or study group the way your child responded to your increased sensitivity. Write your child's response below. If it takes longer than one week to see a change, keep it up!

_____

_____

_____

-11-

COMMUNICATION BRIDGES AND BARRIERS

The Bible discusses a number of bridges and barriers to communication. Four effective bridges to good family communication are:

- the ability to listen to our children
- the ability to feel with our children
- the ability to save our words of encouragement and suggestions for timely moments
- the willingness to be open about our own needs

Three barriers to communicating with our children are:

- nagging
- quarreling
- anger

EXERCISE 1

Our children's talk often contains hidden messages. Their words say one thing, but they may in fact be trying to tell us something quite different from what we hear. Write out the hidden message your child might be trying to give you in the following statements.

1. "Daddy, what can I do?"

_____

_____

2. "I don't feel like eating supper."

_____

_____

3. "Do I have to go to church?"

_____

_____

4. "Billie's parents are getting a divorce."

_____

_____

5. "I just can't stand Mary Ellen and her friends!"

_____

_____

6. "He always gets to do more than I do!"

_____

_____

7. "Dad is always working."

_____

_____

EXERCISE 2

Many communication conflicts are intensified by our failure to freely admit our part in the problem. We find it easier to criticize our children or point out their faults than to be open about our own. First discuss with your spouse or study group what attitude or action of parents might be contributing to the communication problem reflected in each of the statements below. Write your conclusion on the lines below each statement. Then write out what a parent might say to indicate an openness to recognizing her or his part in the problem and a willingness to talk things through.

1. (Teen-ager) "I don't care what you say, I'm going!"

_____

_____

_____

_____

Possible Parent Response:

_____

_____

_____

2. (Junior Higher, slamming the door as she enters her room) "Just leave me alone!"

_____

_____

_____

Possible Parent Response:

_____

_____

_____

3. (Parent) "Don't you sass me like that. I'll slap your face!"

_____

_____

_____

_____

What could this parent have said?

_____

_____

_____

_____

EXERCISE 3

A. Chapter 11 lists seven guidelines that can help us learn to deal with our anger and frustration more constructively. List these guides below.

1. _____

_____

2. _____

_____

3. _____

_____

4. _____

_____

5. _____

_____

6. _____

_____

7. _____

_____

B. Pick a time in the recent past when you lost your temper with one of your children and describe it by answering the following questions.

1. What did your child do that irritated you?

_____

_____

2. What was your mood at the time? (In other words, were you already under a little pressure, uptight, or involved in something else?)

_____

_____

3. Why, do you think, did this particular behavior stir up your anger? (In other words, why are you especially sensitive to this type of behavior?)

_____

_____

4. How did your child respond to your anger (in both behavior and feelings displayed)?

_____

_____

5. Do you see any scriptural principles that could apply to your reaction or to the reasons for your reactions? _____

_____

_____

If so, what are they?

_____

_____

_____

6. How could you have discharged your anger more constructively?

_____

_____

_____

7. What could you do that will help you respond a bit more calmly next time?

_____

_____

_____

-12-

SEX EDUCATION IN THE HOME

For centuries both secular society and the Christian church have held an essentially negative view of human sexuality. This is finally beginning to change. We are talking more freely about our sexual functioning and beginning to see it as a wholesome, natural aspect of life. In spite of this new openness, however, many of us still feel a surge of anxiety when our children ask frank yet innocent questions about sexuality and bodily functions. This chapter is written to help put the process of sex education in its biblical perspective.

EXERCISE 1

Chapter 12 summarizes the biblical view of human sexuality in an eightfold manner. List those eight principles below and write out at least one Scripture verse that supports each statement. You may also want to add other statements on the biblical view of human sexuality on a separate sheet.

    1. Principle: _____

_____

Scripture Reference: _____

_____

_____

2. Principle: _____

Scripture Reference: _____

_____

_____

3. Principle: _____

Scripture Reference: _____

_____

_____

4. Principle: _____

Scripture Reference: _____

_____

_____

5. Principle: _____

Scripture Reference: _____

_____

_____

6. Principle: _____

_____

_____

Scripture Reference: ⎯⎯⎯⎯⎯⎯⎯⎯⎯⎯⎯

⎯⎯⎯⎯⎯⎯⎯⎯⎯⎯⎯⎯⎯⎯⎯⎯⎯⎯⎯⎯⎯⎯⎯⎯

⎯⎯⎯⎯⎯⎯⎯⎯⎯⎯⎯⎯⎯⎯⎯⎯⎯⎯⎯⎯⎯⎯⎯⎯

⎯⎯⎯⎯⎯⎯⎯⎯⎯⎯⎯⎯⎯⎯⎯⎯⎯⎯⎯⎯⎯⎯⎯⎯

7. Principle: ⎯⎯⎯⎯⎯⎯⎯⎯⎯⎯⎯⎯⎯⎯⎯⎯

⎯⎯⎯⎯⎯⎯⎯⎯⎯⎯⎯⎯⎯⎯⎯⎯⎯⎯⎯⎯⎯⎯⎯⎯

Scripture Reference: ⎯⎯⎯⎯⎯⎯⎯⎯⎯⎯⎯

⎯⎯⎯⎯⎯⎯⎯⎯⎯⎯⎯⎯⎯⎯⎯⎯⎯⎯⎯⎯⎯⎯⎯⎯

⎯⎯⎯⎯⎯⎯⎯⎯⎯⎯⎯⎯⎯⎯⎯⎯⎯⎯⎯⎯⎯⎯⎯⎯

⎯⎯⎯⎯⎯⎯⎯⎯⎯⎯⎯⎯⎯⎯⎯⎯⎯⎯⎯⎯⎯⎯⎯⎯

8. Principle: ⎯⎯⎯⎯⎯⎯⎯⎯⎯⎯⎯⎯⎯⎯⎯⎯

⎯⎯⎯⎯⎯⎯⎯⎯⎯⎯⎯⎯⎯⎯⎯⎯⎯⎯⎯⎯⎯⎯⎯⎯

Scripture Reference: ⎯⎯⎯⎯⎯⎯⎯⎯⎯⎯⎯

⎯⎯⎯⎯⎯⎯⎯⎯⎯⎯⎯⎯⎯⎯⎯⎯⎯⎯⎯⎯⎯⎯⎯⎯

⎯⎯⎯⎯⎯⎯⎯⎯⎯⎯⎯⎯⎯⎯⎯⎯⎯⎯⎯⎯⎯⎯⎯⎯

⎯⎯⎯⎯⎯⎯⎯⎯⎯⎯⎯⎯⎯⎯⎯⎯⎯⎯⎯⎯⎯⎯⎯⎯

EXERCISE 2

Our attitudes toward sexuality and sex education are strongly influenced by our upbringing.

A. Describe the attitude toward sexuality and the human body that existed in your childhood homes by completing chart A together, using different color pens.

B. How do you rate your own and your spouse's attitude toward sexuality? Using different color pens, check yes or no in the boxes in chart B to indicate whether or not the statement applies in your situation.

Chart A
FOR HUSBAND AND WIFE

	Yes	No
"My parents spoke freely about the human body and sexual functioning."		
"My parents were open to my questions about sex."		
"My parents freely displayed physical affection for each other and for the children."		
"My parents had frank discussions with me about sex."		
"I grew up knowing that sex was given by God and that there were some constructive guides for expressing it."		
"I find it just as easy to believe God forgives sexual sins as any others."		
"Our bodies and our sexuality were treated as a normal, wholesome aspect of family life."		

EXERCISE 3

Our children's attitudes toward their bodies are shaped by a variety of things: their natural curiosity, peers, schooling, books, and family environment. Discuss with your spouse or study group the various factors that have influenced your children's attitudes toward sexuality. Then briefly describe the attitude toward sexuality you think each of your children has and jot down anything you may be able to do to ensure that the children continue to develop a wholesome attitude in this area. (Use separate sheets as necessary.)

Chart B
FOR HUSBAND AND WIFE

	Yes	No
"We can talk freely about the human body and sexual functioning."		
"We are open to questions about sex."		
"We are a physically affectionate family."		
"Our relationship with one another is enjoyable and good."		
"We have had frank talks about sex with our children."		
"Our children know how their bodies function and understand the process of conception and birth."		
"Our children realize that sex was given by God and that there are some limits to its expression."		
"Our children know that God forgives sexual sins as well as other wrongdoing."		
"In our family our bodies and our sexuality are treated as normal, wholesome aspects of family life."		

Child's attitude:

_____

_____

Ways you can help:

_____

_____

-13-

ACCOUNTABILITY: PARENT AND CHILD

Chapter 13 suggests that parents and their children share the responsibility for children's development and life style. "Even a child is known by his actions" (Prov. 20:11), but parents are also to "train a child in the way he should go" (Prov. 22:6). The parents' responsibility is to provide for children's needs and to train, instruct, and correct the child. Children, however, must also assume a significant measure of responsibility for their choices.

EXERCISE 1

A. Using a different color pen than your spouse list two positive habits, attitudes, or attributes that you learned from your mother.

1. _____

_____

2. _____

_____

B. Using a different color pen than your spouse list two positive habits, attitudes, or attributes that you learned from your father.

1. _____

_____

2. _____

_____

C. List two negative traits that you acquired from your mother.

1. _____

_____

2. _____

_____

D. List two negative traits that you acquired from your father.

1. _____

_____

2. _____

_____

EXERCISE 2

A. For each of your children list two positive and two negative traits she or he is learning from you.

Child

    Positive 1. _____

                2. _____

    Negative 1. _____

                2. _____

B. How do you feel when you see your child developing some of your best characteristics?

_____

_____

_____

C. What can you begin to do about some of the negative traits your children are picking up from you?

_____

_____

_____

EXERCISE 3

Select a problem one of your older children is experiencing and discuss its causes thoroughly. When did it first begin? What part did you play in the development of the problem? Your spouse? Your child? Briefly describe the problem and your conclusions below.

_____

_____

_____

_____

_____

_____

_____

_____

-14-

ΦARENTS
AND THE
EXPERTS

In chapter 14 we look at seven guidelines that can help us determine how scriptural and how helpful a particular book or approach to parenting is. Since no book has all the answers, we can profit from studying several books on parenting. But in doing this we need to be selective. Here are seven key areas to examine when evaluating books and materials for parents:

- The author's attitude toward the Bible
- The consistency and comprehensiveness of the author's use of Scripture
- The author's view of human nature
- The author's position on family government or leadership
- The author's understanding or positive discipline and training
- The author's view on personal (child) and parental responsibility
- The author's sensitivity to *both* parents and children

EXERCISE 1

Following is the family leadership chart discussed in chapter 4 in addition to several excerpts from other books for parents. Read and discuss each quote; then decide whether it reflects a primarily authoritarian, permissive, or loving approach to authority. Since parenting styles range on a continuum these quotes may reflect aspects of more than one parenting style. Similarly, an author may seem to reflect one parenting style when we read one part of the book and another when we read a later part. We need to understand the total approach of an author before evaluating the adequacy of the parenting style being advocated. For now, however, simply select the style that seems to best characterize the selected portion. Consult the chart on parenting styles for help.

> Parents need to be delivered of phony guilt complexes when it comes to disciplining their children. This one simple realization changed the atmosphere of our family overnight. God expects you to spank your children when they rebel or disobey.[1]

Style: _____

Why? _____

_____

_____

_____

_____

> To help our children, then, we must turn from the obsolete autocratic method of demanding submission to a new order based on the principles of freedom and responsibility. Our children no longer can be forced into compliance; they must be stimulated and encour-

---

[1] Larry Christenson, *The Christian Family* (Minneapolis: Bethany Fellowship, 1970), p. 102.

STYLES OF FAMILY LEADERSHIP

	Authoritarian	Permissive	Loving Authority
Primary Focus	External conformity or obedience	Attitudes	Attitudes that result in proper behavior
Use of Parental Authority and Power	Unquestioning use	Not used	Carried out as a delegated responsibility from the Lord
Motivation	Fear, pressure, power, and coercion	Love, stimulation, and cooperation	Love, stimulation, cooperation, and appropriate correction or use of consequences
View of Human Nature	Basically sinful	Basically good	Image-bearers, yet sinful
Attitude Toward Child	Children to be seen and not heard	Children to be trusted implicitly and respected	Children to be deeply respected as creations of God but also recognized as being sinful and having rebellious tendencies
Resulting Behavior	Blind conformity or rebellion	Insufficient controls or search for limits	Balance of cooperativeness, conformity, and creative assertiveness
Resulting Emotions	Fear, guilt, or resentment	A level of self-respect because of parental trust, but anxiety or insecurity because of lack of limits	Self-respect accompanied by security and love

aged into voluntarily taking their part in the mainte-
nance of order.[2]

Style: _____

Why? _____

_____

_____

_____

Early in our parenthood we took the pledge—*no
spanking!* And to be sure we wouldn't turn back we
said to our small fry, "You hear this! We are through
forever with swatting and switching and all general
clobbering. There has to be some better way than bare
hands on bare derriere. We don't know for sure what,
but we'll work out something together. And whatever
it is, it won't be physical. So, we kid you not, if ever
we start to hit, you run like crazy. We've gone
temporarily out of our minds."[3]

Style: _____

Why? _____

_____

_____

_____

What is it that moves you, dear reader, to live a holy
life? What is it that stirs you to obey the Lord's
commands? Isn't it the fear of God? I hope so. . . .
Love may make you *desire* to obey the Lord, but it is
FEAR that *prods* you to do it.[4]

[2] Rudolf Dreikurs, *Children: The Challenge* (New York: Hawthorn
Books, 1964), p. 10.
[3] Charlie Shedd, *You Can Be a Great Parent* (Waco, Texas: Word
Books, 1970), p. 43.
[4] C. S. Lovett, *What's a Parent to Do?* (Baldwin Park, Calif.: Personal
Christianity, 1971), p. 64.

Style: _____

Why? _____

_____

_____

_____

_____

When a parent loses the early confrontation with the child, the later conflicts become harder to win. The parent who never wins, who is too weak or too tired or too busy to win, is making a costly mistake that will come back to haunt him during the child's adolescence. If you can't make a five-year-old pick up his toys, it is unlikely that you will exercise any impressive degree of control during his adolescence, the most defiant time of life.[5]

Style: _____

Why? _____

_____

_____

_____

_____

The central goal of disciplinary methods is to incite the child to be readily willing to obey parental commands and to heed instruction. When a child is motivated to obey willingly, he develops a character structure in which he wholeheartedly wants to do what is right because he enjoys being right.[6]

Style: _____

[5] James Dobson, *Dare to Discipline* (Wheaton, Ill.: Tyndale House, 1970), p. 19.
[6] Maurice Wagner, *The Sensation of Being Somebody* (Grand Rapids: Zondervan, 1975), p. 76.

Why? _____

_____

_____

_____

_____

_____

> My own conviction is that as more people begin to
> understand power and authority more completely and
> accept its use as unethical, more parents will apply
> those understandings to adult-child relationships; will
> begin to feel that it is just as immoral in those
> relationships; and then will be forced to search for
> creative new non-power methods that all adults can
> use with children and youth.[7]

Style: _____

Why? _____

_____

_____

_____

_____

_____

EXERCISE 2

Here are some statements that show various authors' views
of human nature. Below each quotation tell whether it fits
with the biblical view of children as image-bearing yet
sinful. Also tell whether is emphasizes either human
sinfulness or human goodness at the expense of the other.

> Since the time of the French Revolution the idea has
> gained wide acceptance that human nature is basically

[7]Thomas Gordon, *Parent Effectiveness Training* (New York: New
American Library, Plume Books, 1975), p. 191.

good. The "evil" that crops out from time to time is due to lack of education and understanding, or perhaps from psychological patterns inflicted by one's background and environment. What is needed, we are told, is education and perhaps some adjustment in one's environment—economic, social, political, psychological. Once a person "understands" and once artificial restrictions have been removed, the innate goodness of human nature will burst into flower. The Bible comes at the business of child-raising from a fundamentally different point of view. The Bible does not look upon a child as basically good! "Behold, I was brought forth in iniquity, and in sin my mother conceived me" (Psalm 51:5). The Bible does not view a child as one who essentially wants to do the wise and right thing. Its understanding of the child's nature is different and therefore its approach to discipline is different. "Folly is bound up in the heart of a child, but the rod of discipline drives it from him" (Proverbs 22:5). The Scriptural method of discipline is simple and unequivocal: the rod.[8]

Let us lay it down as an incontestable principle that the first impulses of nature are always right. There is no original perversity in the human heart. Of every vice we say how it entered and whence it came.[9]

---

[8] Larry Christenson, *The Christian Family* (Minneapolis: Bethany Fellowship, 1970), p. 95.

[9] Jean Jacques Rousseau, *The Émile*, trans. and ed. William Boyd (New York: Teacher's College Press, Columbia University, 1962), p. 104.

First, every child has bents or tendencies toward good. There are certain characteristics woven into the inner fabric of each child that give his physical features, emotions, basic personality, interests, and abilities. We'll call these tendencies the "good bents."
. . . They are productive and beneficial to the child and the world he enters.

Second, every child has bents or tendencies toward evil. There are certain characteristics within every child that inevitably result in conflict, heartache, anxiety, and selfishness.[10]

---

[10]Charles Swindoll, *You and Your Child* (Nashville: Thomas Nelson, 1977), p. 28.

WHERE DO WE GO FROM HERE?

Congratulations! You made it! Many people who begin a study like this never make it through to the end. The fact that you did shows a strong commitment to being the kind of parent God intends you to be. But, as you well know, becoming a better parent is an ongoing process. We learn more quickly in some areas than others. This chapter is designed to give you a chance to review some of the most significant aspects of your recent study of the biblical model of parenting and to look ahead to other areas you may wish to study or to work on further.

EXERCISE 1

New insights, new habits, and new ways of looking at things are reinforced by reflection and review. To help you retain the material in your recent study, complete the blanks below.

A. What specific new *biblical* insights or scriptural principles did you learn during your study?

_____

_____

_____

_____

_____

B. List at least two other important things you learned.

_____

_____

_____

_____

_____

C. As a result of your study are you now doing anything differently than you did before you started? _____ If so, list specific examples:

_____

_____

_____

_____

D. If you answered yes to the question above, how are your children responding to your changes? (Be as specific as possible.)

_____

_____

_____

_____

_____

_____

EXERCISE 2

Sometimes we see the need to apply a certain insight or principle, but we have difficulty putting it into practice. List below a few principles of parenting covered in this study that you would like to see worked out more consistently in your life.

1. _____

_____

2. _____

_____

3. _____

_____

4. _____

_____

5. _____

_____

EXERCISE 3

This study has focused on the biblical pattern of parenting. In the future you may want to go on and study other aspects of parenting not dealt with in detail here or to some more specific applications of these basic principles. In case you do, check the topics below that interest you the most.

_____ Communication

_____ Sex education

_____ Discipline

_____ Building Self-esteem

_____ Other

₵NOTES

Chapter 1

[1]Benjamin Spock, *Baby and Child Care* (New York: Pocket Books, 1957).

[2]Included here are books such as *How to Raise Your Children for Christ*, Andrew Murray (Minneapolis: Bethany Fellowship, 1975); *You and Your Child*, Charles Swindoll (Nashville: Thomas Nelson Publishers, 1977); *You the Parent*, Lawrence Richards (Chicago: Moody Bible Institute, 1974) and *The Christian Family*, Larry Christenson (Minneapolis: Bethany Fellowship, 1970).

[3]Included here are books such as *Dare to Discipline*, James Dobson (Wheaton: Tyndale Publishers, 1970); *The People You Live With*, Quentin Hyder (Old Tappan, New Jersey: Fleming H. Revell Co., 1975); *Christian Child Rearing and Personality Development*, Paul Meier (Grand Rapids: Baker Book House, 1977); and my own *Help! I'm a Parent* (Grand Rapids: Zondervan Publishing House, 1972).

[4]Al Fabrizio and Pat Fabrizio, *Children—Fun or Frenzy?* (Palo Alto, Calif.: Alegria Press, 1969).

[5]John Gill, *A Body of Divinity*, 2 vols. (1839; repr. ed., Grand Rapids: Baker Book House, 1978).

[6]Herbert Lockyer, *All the Children of the Bible* (Grand Rapids: Zondervan Publishing House, 1970).

[7]Gill, *Body of Divinity*, p. 2:729.

[8]Throughout the history of the Christian church, doctrine has been formulated and systematized in response to the cultural needs and the conflicts of the day. As Berkhof put it in his *History of Christian Doctrine* (Grand Rapids: Baker Book House, 1975), p. 19: "In the history of Dogma we see the church becoming ever increasingly conscious of the riches of divine truth under the guidance of the Holy Spirit, mindful of her high prerogative as the pillar and ground of the truth, and engaged in the defense of the faith once delivered to the saints."

It wasn't until the Reformation, for example, that a great deal of attention was given to biblical anthropology. And it wasn't until the last century that more detailed studies of eschatology began to play a significant role in theology. Perhaps the widespread current interest in the family is finally providing the stimulus needed to develop a theology of parenting and to include this essential area in our theological studies.

Chapter 2

[1]Developing a theology of parenting could be approached from the perspective of historical theology, biblical theology, or systematic theology. In historical theology we would review and evaluate the teachings on the family, including the theological conceptions of parenting, that have been

constructed throughout the Christian era. However, earlier theologians' lack of interest in parenting makes this of little value to us today. If we were to choose the method of biblical theology, we would begin with Genesis and move through the Bible taking careful note of the setting and of the ways in which God revealed Himself in different ages. This approach has a great deal to commend it because there is a steady unfolding of God's design for the family. And the historical settings of the Bible do add substantially to our understanding and appreciation of God's plan.

I have chosen, however, to approach the subject from the viewpoint of systematic theology. Because it organizes biblical truth by topics, it seems to offer the most effective method of treating the full range of biblical teachings that relate to parenting. Although much of the material in a theology of parenting such as this deals with the areas of theology proper and of biblical anthropology, its distinctive qualities and contributions merit separate consideration.

[2]Richard Strauss, *Confident Children and How They Grow* (Wheaton: Tyndale House Publishers, 1975), p. 23.

[3]Herbert Lockyer, *All the Children of the Bible* (Grand Rapids: Zondervan Publishing House, 1970), p. 73.

[4]This, of course, takes us into the study of theology proper. Although we will not go into great detail in this area, in chapter nine we will look briefly at some of the attributes of God that relate to parenting.

[5]Biblical anthropology is probably the area of traditional systematic theology with the greatest relevance for a theology of parenting.

Chapter 3

[1]For example, Isaiah 48:11; 60:21; Ezekiel 36:22-25; 39:7; 1 Corinthians 15:24-28; Ephesians 1:4-6; 3:9-12; Revelation 4:11.

[2]A. H. Strong, *Systematic Theology* (New York: Fleming H. Revell, 1907), p. 400.

[3]Herbert Lockyer, *All the Children of the Bible* (Grand Rapids: Zondervan Publishing House, 1970), p. 22.

[4]Lockyer, *Children of the Bible*, p. 23.

[5]Erich Sauer, *The King of the Earth* (Grand Rapids: Wm. B. Eerdmans Publishing Company, 1962), p. 72. Sauer also wrote: "If we are to understand the purpose and goal of man's creation, we must see them from the perspective of eternity before the universe, and above all, before the earth came into being. From this standpoint we shall learn to see him as a kingly instrument in the hand of the Creator for the transfiguration of the world of nature. We shall see him also as a vessel for divine grace and glory, called to worship, to conformity to God's image, to be a son of God, through His creation, and to the vocation of ruler through eternity" (ibid., p. 11).

[6]Richard Strauss, *Confident Children and How They Grow* (Wheaton: Tyndale House Publishers, 1975), pp. 23-24.

[7]B. B. Warfield states: "But it is so characteristic of our Lord's teaching that it may fairly be said that the family was to His mind the nearest of

human analogies to the order that obtains in the kingdom of God, and the picture which he draws of the relations that exist between God and His people is largely only a 'transfiguration of the family!'" *Hastings' Dictionary of the New Testament*, J. Hastings, ed. (Grand Rapids: Baker Book House, 1973), s.v. "Children."

Chapter 4

[1]C. S. Lovett, *What's A Parent To Do?* (Baldwin Park, California: Personal Christianity, 1971), p. 88.

[2]A. S. Neill, *Summerhill: A Radical Approach to Child Rearing* (New York: Hart Publishing Company, 1960), p. 114.

[3]Larry Christenson, *The Christian Family* (Minneapolis: Bethany Fellowship, 1970), p. 95.

[4]Ibid., p. 112.

[5]Neil, *Summerhill*, p. 104.

[6]Jean Jacques Rousseau, *The Émile*, trans. and ed. William Boyd (New York: Teachers' College Press, Columbia University, 1962), pp. 37-38.

[7]Ibid., p. 40.

[8]Rudolf Dreikurs, *The Challenge of Child Training* (New York: Hawthorne Books, 1972), p. 29.

[9]Ibid., p. 152.

[10]Thomas Gordon, *Parent Effectiveness Training* (New York: New American Library, 1975), p. 164.

[11]Louis Berkhof, *Manual of Christian Doctrine* (Grand Rapids: Wm. B. Eerdmans Publishing Company, 1933), p. 127.

[12]H. C. Thiessen, *Lectures in Systematic Theology* (Grand Rapids: Wm. B. Eerdmans Publishing Company, 1949), pp. 219-22.

[13]B. B. Warfield, *Dictionary of the New Testament* , James Hastings, ed. (Grand Rapids: Baker Book House, 1973), s.v. "Children."

[14]Historian R. R. Palmer describes the impact that Christianity has had on respect for human life as follows: "It is impossible to exaggerate the importance of the coming of Christianity. It brought with it . . . an altogether new sense of human life. Where the Greeks had shown man his mind, the Christians showed him his soul; and they taught that in the sight of God all souls were equal, and that every human life was sacrosanct and inviolate. . . . Where the Greeks had identified the beautiful and the good, had thought ugliness to be bad, and had shrunk from disease and imperfection and from everything misshapen as horrible and repulsive, the Christians . . . sought out the diseased, the crippled, and the mutilated to give them help. Love, for the ancients, was never quite distinguished from Venus; for the Christians, who held that God was love, it took on deep overtones of sacrifice and compassion." In *A History of the Modern World* (New York: Alfred A. Knopf, 1953), p. 11.

[15]Francis Schaeffer, *Genesis in Space and Time* (Downers Grove: Inter-Varsity Press, 1972), p. 54.

[16]Whether the essence of this sin is selfishness as Strong suggests *(Sys-*

tematic Theology), lack of conformity to the law of God as Hodge maintains (*Outlines of Theology*), or not conforming to the character of God as Chafer (*Systematic Theology*) and Buswell (*Basic Christian Doctrines*) state, is not as relevant to the task of child rearing as the fact that sin has become a central dynamic in every person's life—including children.

[17]For a good discussion of the early denial of the sinfulness of man in Pelagianism, see Philip Schaff, *History of the Christian Church* (Grand Rapids: Wm. B. Eerdmans Publishing Company, 1910), pp. 785–843.

[18]As A. A. Hodge put it: "Inability [to please God] consists, not in the loss of any faculty of the soul, nor in the loss of free agency, for the sinner determines his own acts, nor in the mere disinclination to what is good. It arises from want of spiritual discernment, and hence want of proper affections. Inability belongs only to the things of the Spirit. What man cannot do is to repent, believe, regenerate himself. He cannot put forth any act which merits the approbation of God. Sin cleaves to all he does and from its dominion he cannot free himself." In *Systematic Theology* (New York: Fleming H. Revell, 1907), p. 643.

And as G. C. Berkouwer comments on the tendency of some to misstate the concept of depravity in a way that denies to humankind anything but an outward appearance of good: "Such an explanation is generally not attempted, and when it is presented, it can never be convincing. Anyone who attempts to combat humanism in this way must necessarily underestimate the actuality of God's gifts on fallen man, however much he feels he is basing his view on the doctrine of total corruption." In *Man: The Image of God*, Studies in Dogmatics (Grand Rapids: Wm. B. Eerdmans Publishing Co., 1962), p. 186.

[19]Stanley Coopersmith, *Antecedents of Self-Esteem* (San Francisco: W. H. Freeman & Co., 1967).

Chapter 5

[1]Margaret Ribble's report on the infant disease marasmus makes it clear that infants need love and affection. Commenting on infants mysteriously wasting away and dying, she writes: "The astonishing discovery was made that babies in the best homes and hospitals, given the most careful physical attention, sometimes drifted into the condition of slow dying, while infants in the poorest homes, with a loving mother, often overcame the handicaps of poverty and unhygienic surroundings and became bouncing babies. It was found that the element lacking in the sterilized lives of the babies of the former class, and generously supplied to those that flourished in spite of hit or miss environmental conditions, was mother love." In *The Rights of Infants* (New York: Columbia University Press, 1965), p. 4.

[2]Nathan Stone, *Names of God in the Old Testament* (Chicago: Moody Press, 1944), p. 27. See also Andrew Jukes, *The Names of God* (Grand Rapids: Kregel Publications, 1967), pp. 64, 66.

Harold B. Kuhn, among others, questions this interpretation: "This seems to rest upon a confusion upon the part of a translator of the LXX, who incorrectly associated the word *sadu* with the term meaning 'breast.' The correct understanding of the name, as being derived from the name mountain seems to suggest strength, stability, and permanence. It has been suggested that the name is basically poetic, thus indicating majestic stability, the reliable refuge, the unmoved pillar." In *The Zondervan Pictorial Encyclopedia of the Bible*, Merill C. Tenney, ed. (Grand Rapids: Zondervan Publishing House, 1975), s.v. "God, Names of."

Whether or not El Shaddai connotes supplying, the bulk of Scripture certainly portrays God as the One who nourishes and supplies His children's needs.

[3]Maurice Wagner, *The Sensation of Being Somebody* (Grand Rapids: Zondervan Publishing House, 1975), p. 164.

Chapter 6

[1]A. H. Strong marks this distinction clearly when he writes: "The object of penalty is not the reformation of the offender or the insuring of social or governmental safety. These ends may be incidentally secured through its infliction, but the great end of penalty is the vindication of the character of the law-giver. Penalty is essentially a necessary reaction of the divine holiness against sin. Punishment is essentially different from chastisement [discipline]. The latter proceeds from love (Jer. 10:24—'Correct me, but in measure, not in thine anger'; Heb. 12:6—'Whom the Lord loveth He chasteneth'). Punishment proceeds not from love but from justice (see Exod. 20:22—'I shall have executed judgments in her, and shall be sanctified in her . . .')." In *Systematic Theology* (New York: Fleming H. Revell, 1907), p. 653.

[2]See also Matthew 25:46; 2 Peter 2:9; and Revelation 16:1–7.

[3]W. E. Vine, in commenting on the use of *kólasis* (punishment or torment) in this verse, says, "This kind of fear is expelled by perfect love; where God's love is being perfected in us, it gives no room for the fear of meeting with His reprobation." In *Expository Dictionary of New Testament Words* (Westwood, N.J.: Fleming H. Revell Company, 1940).

[4]Charles Swindoll, *You and Your Child* (Nashville: Thomas Nelson, 1977), p. 18.

[5]J. P. Lange, ed., *Lange's Commentary on the Holy Scriptures*, 12 vols. (Grand Rapids: Zondervan Publishing House, 1960), 5:192. In commenting on the merits of interpreting "in his way" as referring to one specific or right direction, Lange says that although this interpretation "has been generally adopted and used where little account is made of the original [language], it has the least support from the Hebrew idiom." Ibid.

Crawford H. Toy comments: "Train up—give instruction, experience. In the way he is to go, literally according to his way, that is, not exactly 'in the path of industry and piety' (which would require in the right way) nor 'according to the bodily and mental development of the child' (which does not agree with the second clause) but 'in accordance with the manner of life to which he is destined.'" In *A Critical and Exegetical Commentary on the*

Book of Proverbs, The International Critical Commentary, S. R. Driver, A. Plummer, and C. A. Briggs, eds. (Edinburgh: T. and T. Clark, 1899), p. 415.

⁶J. Denny states: "The etymological connection of these words with [*pais*] suggests that education in the widest sense of the word, including reference to the means as well as the end of the process, is the main idea involved." In *Dictionary of the Bible*, James Hastings, ed. (New York: Charles Scribner's Sons, 1898), s.v. "Chastening."

P. E. Dovers writes: "In the Bible discipline is closely associated with training, instruction, and knowledge on the one hand and with reproof, correction, and punishment on the other hand. In the New Testament use of [*paideia*](discipline) and [*paideuo*] ('to instruct, educate, discipline'), the Jewish tradition comes in contact with the broader educational ideal of Greece. In the world of the Greeks these terms were applied to the household training of children and also to man's training to take his place in the culture of the world—with little emphasis on chastisement." In *The Interpreter's Dictionary of the Bible*, G. A. Buttrick, et al. eds. (Nashville: Abingdon Press, 1962), s.v. "Discipline.")

⁷Two helpful books on conversational prayer for families are Rosalind Rinker's *Prayer: Conversing With God* (Grand Rapids: Zondervan Publishing House, 1959), and *How to Have Family Prayers* (Grand Rapids: Zondervan Publishing House, 1977).

Chapter 7

¹The Book of Proverbs makes frequent use of *musar*. From verses 2 and 3 of chapter 24 *musar* is a recurring theme. As with *yasar*, the Scripture uses *musar* to convey a breadth of meaning relating to correcting, discipline, and instruction. *Musar* also occurs in the following passages in Proverbs: 1:2, 3, 7, 8; 3:11; 4:1; 5:12; 8:10, 33; 10:17; 13:18; 15:15, 32; 19:20, 27; 23:13, 23; 24:32.

²Here we see that Scripture utilized the concept of "natural consequences" long before Rudolf Dreikurs, in the footsteps of Rousseau and Adler, popularized it in *Children: The Challenge* (New York: Hawthorn Books, 1964). The problem with Dreikurs's use of natural consequences is that since he sees humanity as essentially good and recommends a totally democratic style of family government, he believes natural, logical consequences and a family council can totally remove the need for parental authority and forms of discipline such as spanking.

³There is another lesson in this story—the resentment of the older son. We will not develop it here, except to note that the child who appears well adjusted may harbor some very sinful attitudes.

Chapter 8

¹As Lewis Sperry Chafer wrote: "Since law and grace are opposed to each other at every point, it is impossible for them to co-exist, either as the

ground of acceptance before God or as the rule of life." In *Grace: The Glorious Theme* (Grand Rapids: Dunham Publishing Company, 1922), p. 215.

[2]Ibid., pp. 236–237.

[3]Similarly, this does not mean there was no grace during Old Testament times. The call of Abraham and the sovereign election of Israel to be God's chosen people are manifestations of God's grace. Grace did exist before the Cross, but it had not been illuminated and demonstrated by the love that sent Jesus to the cross.

[4]J. F. Strombeck, *Disciplined by Grace* (Moline, Ill.: Strombeck Agency, 1946), pp. 96-97.

[5]Ibid., p. 95.

[6]There is, of course, the awesome respect for a holy God. But this is entirely different from the fear of God's wrath and punishment that were forever banished from the Christian's life through Christ's death at Calvary.

Chapter 9

[1]Andrew Murray, *How to Raise Your Children for Christ* (Minneapolis: Bethany Fellowship, 1975), p. 17.

[2]Ibid.

[3]Richard Strauss, *Confident Children and How They Grow* (Wheaton, Ill.: Tyndale House Publishers, 1975), pp. 23-24.

[4]Roland Fleck, Larry Day, and Wes Riley, "Concept of God and Parental Images as a Function of Age of Christian Conversion Experience," paper presented at the 1974 convention of the Christian Association for Psychological Studies.

[5]Mark Keyser and Gary Collins, "Parental Image and the Concept of God: An Evangelical Protestant-Catholic Comparison," *Journal of Psychology and Theology*, 2, no. 1, pp. 69-80.

[6]J. B. Phillips, *Your God Is Too Small* (New York: Macmillan Company, 1969), pp. 14-15.

[7]Wendell Robley and Grace Robley, *Spank Me If You Love Me* (Harrison, Ark.: New Leaf Press, 1976), p. 19.

[8]Ibid., p. 20.

[9]Charles Wesley, "Jesus, Lover of My Soul."

[10]Phillips, *Your God Is Too Small*, p. 32.

[11]This is especially true of God's absolute or immanent attributes such as spirituality, infinity, and perfection.

[12]Besides what is given in this section, passages referring to God's holiness and righteousness are: Exodus 15:11; Deuteronomy 4:8; Psalm 22:3; 47:8; 48:10; 71:15; 96:13; 111:3; Isaiah 6:3; 57:15; Jeremiah 23:9; John 17:11, 24-26; Acts 17:31; Romans 3:25-26; Revelation 16:5. Other verses challenging us to holiness and righteousness are Romans 6:12-13; 1 Thessalonians 4:7; and Hebrews 12:14.

[13]C. H. Thiessen, *Lectures In Systematic Theology* (Grand Rapids: Wm. B. Eerdmans Publishing Company, 1949), p. 128.

¹⁴Ibid., p. 129.

¹⁵Besides what is given in this section, passages referring to God's love are: Psalm 92:2; Isaiah 63:7; Jeremiah 31:3; John 3:16; Romans 8:35; and Ephesians 3:18-19. Other passages challenging us to love are: John 15:12; 1 Corinthians 13; 16:14; Galatians 5:22; 1 Timothy 1:5; Titus 2:3-4; and 1 John 4:21.

¹⁶Besides what is given in this section, passages referring to God's fairness are: Jeremiah 32:18-19 and Revelation 15:3. Another passage challenging us to deal in fairness is 1 Timothy 5:21.

¹⁷Besides what is given in this section, passages referring to God's sensitivity and gentleness are: John 13:23; 1 Corinthians 10:13; and 1 Peter 3:8. Another passage challenging us to sensitivity and gentleness is 2 Corinthians 10:1.

¹⁸Robert Jamieson, A. R. Fausset, and David Brown, *Commentary on the Whole Bible*, rev. ed. (Grand Rapids: Zondervan Publishing House, 1961), p. 1407.

¹⁹Besides what is given in this section, passages referring to this attribute are: Proverbs 15:33; 16:18-19; 22:4; Matthew 5:3; Philippians 2:5-8; Colossians 3:12; and 1 Peter 5:5.

²⁰Besides what is given in this section, passages referring to these attributes are: Numbers 14:18; Psalm 86:15; Ecclesiastes 7:8; Romans 3:25; and 2 Timothy 2:24.

²¹Besides what is given in this section, another passage referring to God's encouragement of His children is Philippians 2:1.

²²Besides what is given in this section, another passage referring to God's forgiveness is Luke 23:34.

²³Besides what is given in this section, passages referring to these characteristics are: Psalm 89:2; 111:7-8; 132:11; Lamentations 3:23; 1 Thessalonians 5:24; and Hebrews 10:23. Another passage challenging us to live faithfully is 1 Timothy 3:11.

Chapter 10

¹Dorothy Briggs, *Your Child's Self-Esteem* (New York: Doubleday and Company, 1970), p. 2.

²James Dobson, *Hide or Seek* (Old Tappan, N. J.: Fleming H. Revell Company, 1974), p. 12.

³William Homan, *Child Sense* (New York: Bantam Books, 1969), p. 244.

⁴Walter Trobisch, *Love Yourself* (Downers Grove, Ill.: InterVarsity Press, 1976), p. 11.

⁵Robert Schuller, *Self-Love* (New York: Hawthorn Books, 1969), p. 21.

⁶Two notable exceptions to this proof-texting approach are Anthony Hoekema's *The Christian Looks at Himself* (Grand Rapids: Wm. B. Eerdmans, 1975) and Maurice Wagner's *Sensation of Being Somebody* (Grand Rapids: Zondervan, 1975).

⁷See also Bruce Narramore and Bill Counts, *Freedom From Guilt* (Santa Ana, Calif.: Vision House Publishers, 1974), pp. 44-51.

[8]Francis Schaeffer, *Genesis in Space and Time* (Downers Grove, Ill.: InterVarsity Press, 1972), p. 48.

[9]Erich Sauer, *The King of the Earth* (Grand Rapids: Wm. B. Eerdmans Publishing Company, 1972), p. 92.

[10]B. B. Warfield, in *Hastings' Dictionary of the New Testament*, James Hastings, ed. (Grand Rapids: Baker Book House, 1973), s.v. "Children."

[11]Carl F. H. Henry put it this way: "The fall of man is not destructive of the formal image (man's personality) although it involves the distortion (though not demolition) of the material content of the image." In *Baker's Dictionary of Theology*, Everett Harrison, ed. (Grand Rapids: Baker Book House, 1960), s.v. "Man."

Chapter 11

[1]See Norman Wright's *Communication: Key to Your Marriage* (Glendale, Calif.: Regal Books, 1974) for a practical Christian guide to family communication. Haim Ginott's *Between Parent and Child* (New York: Macmillan Company, 1965) is an excellent secular text on parent communication. Ginott's book suffers from a weak approach to discipline that is based on his humanistic assumptions, but it contains much very helpful material for parents.

[2]Cecil Osborne, *The Art of Learning to Love Yourself* (Grand Rapids: Zondervan Publishing House, 1976), p. 78.

Chapter 12

[1]Dwight H. Small, *Christian: Celebrate Your Sexuality* (Old Tappan, N.J.: Fleming H. Revell Company, 1974), p. 46.

[2]Ibid., p. 49.

[3]Ibid., p. 84. Small is also careful to point out that such negative attitudes did not originate in the church but were largely reflections of the culture and philosophy of their day.

[4]Robert Jamieson, A. R. Fausset, and David Brown, *Commentary on the Whole Bible* (Grand Rapids: Zondervan Publishing House, 1961), p. 488.

[5]H. H. Rowley, "The Interpretation of the Song of Songs," in *The Servant of the Lord and Other Essays* (London: Lutterworth, 1952).

[6]J. Sidlow Baxter, *Explore the Book* (Grand Rapids: Zondervan Publishing House, 1960), vol. 3, p. 172.

[7]Joseph Dillow, *Solomon On Sex* (New York: Thomas Nelson, 1977), p. 9.

[8]David Hubbard, in *The New Bible Dictionary* (Grand Rapids: Eerdmans Publishing Co., 1962), J. D. Douglas, ed., s.v. "Song of Solomon."

[9]Baxter, *Explore The Book*, p. 173.

[10]Scofield writes: "The book is the expression of pure marital love as ordained by God in creation, and the vindication of that love as against both asceticism and lust. . . . Its interpretation is three-fold: (1) as a vivid unfolding of Solomon's love for a Shulamite girl; (2) as a figurative revelation of

God's love for His covenant people, Israel, the wife of the Lord (Isa. 54:5-6; Jer. 2:2; Ezek. 16:8-14, 20-21, 32, 38; Hos. 2:16, 18-20); and (3) as an allegory of Christ's love for His heavenly bride, the church (2 Cor. 11:1-2; Eph. 5:25-32). (In C. I. Scofield, ed., *The New Scofield Reference Bible* [New York: Oxford University Press, 1967], p. 705.)

[11]Among the helpful Christian publications on sexuality are *The Act of Marriage*, by Tim LaHaye (Grand Rapids: Zondervan Publishing House, 1976) and *Intended for Pleasure*, by Ed Wheat (Old Tappan, N. J.: Fleming H. Revell, 1977).

[12]Brown, Driver, and Briggs suggest that "vulva" is the preferred translation. In F. H. W. Gesenius, *A Hebrew and English Lexicon of the Old Testament*, ed. Francis Brown, S. R. Driver, and Charles A. Briggs (London: Oxford University Press, 1966).

[13]Helpful books for parents on sex education include *Sex Is a Parent Affair*, by Letha Scanzoni (Glendale: Regal Books, 1973) and *From Parent to Child About Sex*, by Wilson Grant (Grand Rapids: Zondervan Publishing House, 1973).

Chapter 13

[1]Charles Swindoll, *You and Your Child* (Nashville: Thomas Nelson Publishers, 1977), p. 36.

Chapter 14

[1]Al Fabrizio and Pat Fabrizio, *Children: Fun or Frenzy?* (Palo Alto, Calif.: Alegria Press, 1969), p. 10.

[2]Howard Hendricks, *Heaven Help the Home!* (Wheaton Ill.: Victor Books, 1974), p. 67.

[3]C. S. Lovett, *What's a Parent to Do?* (Baldwin Park, Calif.: Personal Christianity, 1971), p. 61.

[4]H. Werner, "Wise Parental Love" in *The Marriage Affair*, J. Allan Petersen, ed. (Wheaton, Ill.: Tyndale, 1971), pp. 161-62.

[5]James Dobson, *Dare to Discipline* (Wheaton, Ill.: Tyndale House, 1970), p. 13.

[6]Lawrence Richard, *You The Parent* (Chicago: Moody Press, 1974), pp. 76-77.

[7]I suggest, for instance, that Bill Gothard's concepts in his Basic Youth Conflicts seminars should not be adopted uncritically. Although the seminars embody a great deal of biblical truth and have without any doubt helped many, Gothard's concept of "chain of command," the nature of and response to authority, and methods of changing behavior (which border on legalism) should be carefully scrutinized in the light of Scripture as a whole.

[8]Here I would include books such as Haim Ginott's *Between Parent and Child* (New York: MacMillan Company, 1965), Rudolf Dreikurs's *Children: The Challenge* (New York: Hawthorn Books, 1974), and Dorothy Briggs's

Your Child's Self-Esteem (New York: Doubleday and Company, 1970). All of these books reflect a sensitive understanding of children that parents need. They run counter to biblical truth, however, in several points relating to the nature of man, discipline, and family government. I believe that Thomas Gordon's *Parent Effectiveness Training* (New York: Peter H. Wyden, 1971) so blatantly rejects the biblical view of both man and family government that I hesitate to recommend it, though it does contain much helpful input for readers who have time to ferret out truth from error.

[9]Jay Adams, *The Christian Counselor's Manual* (Grand Rapids: Baker Book House, 1972), p. 82.

[10]Adams also writes: "Skinner's basic presupposition that man is only another animal means that he too has devised a methodology growing out of this assumption and that, therefore, cannot be eclectically borrowed and used by Christian counselors" (*The Big Umbrella*, Baker Book House, 1972, p. 131). Adams also says: "James Dobson's book, *Dare to Discipline*, while placing needed emphasis upon discipline by structure is based upon this non-Christian ideology (behaviorism). It is basically a godless humanistic book. The discipline advocated is behavioristic (Skinnerian). According to Dobson, a child is to be 'trained' as one would train his dog. The methodology does not differ. The presupposition is that man is but another animal."

[11]Francis Schaeffer, *Back to Freedom and Dignity* (Downers Grove, Ill.: InterVarsity Press, 1972), p. 36.

[12]One very helpful book from this perspective is *Living With Children: New Methods for Parents and Teachers*, by Gerald Patterson and Elizabeth Gullion (Champaign, Ill.: Research Press, 1968). It does, however, minimize the role of corrective discipline.

[13]Skinner, for example, writes: "What is being abolished is autonomous man—the inner man, the homunculus man, the possessing demon, the man defended by the literatures of freedom and dignity. His abolition has long been overdue. Autonomous man is a device used to explain what we cannot explain in any other way. He has been constructed from our ignorance and as our understanding increases the very stuff of which he is composed vanishes. Science does not dehumanize man, it dehomunculizes him, and it must be so if it is to prevent the abolition of the human species. To man *qua* man we readily say good riddance. Only by dispossessing him can we turn to the real causes of human behavior. Only then can we turn from the inferred to the observed, from the miraculous to the natural, from the inaccessible to the manipulable." In *Beyond Freedom and Dignity* (New York: Alfred A. Knopf, 1971, pp. 200-201.)

(For ease of reading, notes for the exercise chapters can be found at the bottom of each page.)